En(

Michael experienced success in business leadership and management early. He then took his passion for excellence and has impacted hundreds of small businesses across America. Some of the statements about his consulting and teaching from leaders include:

"Michael had a bigger impact on our production than any other training we've ever exposed to our people. Plus, it had a lasting impact. It was the wisest decision our company ever made."

KEITH PROVANCE — CEO,
Eagle Communications International

"Michael has had a tremendous impact on our people both in productivity and personally. We've had a 30% increase in sales. After 21 years I wish everyone in this industry could be exposed to his teaching."

JERRY TRAMONTOZZI — GM of auto dealership

"Michael's teaching helped our people overcome their fears and keep trying. Their production dramatically increased, they're happier and spending more time in the field prospecting."

GARY CARPENTER — Real Estate Sales Manager

"Since Michael's teaching I've been able to accomplish more in one day than I used to in three. My attitude has turned 180° degrees. The negativity I encounter throughout the day no longer gets me down."

TIM CELESTINO — Stock Broker

"If you miss the opportunity to hear Michael's teaching you will miss a lifetime treat. It's the greatest training I've ever taken. It has changed my life."

ROSETTA MORRIS—Real Estate Agent

"Michael's instruction and teaching are lacking nothing to build a more profitable life and career!"

TIM SMITH — Real Estate Agent

"Michael's teaching is the most balanced I've ever experienced. The very nature of his training demanded that we get personally involved and therefore caused change in the areas of our life which needed improvement."

RAY SNOKE — Real Estate Agent

"Michael's instruction was the turning point of my life. I went from out of control to a man who took control of his life!"

GEORGE TRUBACHIK — Auto Repair Owner

"Michael's guidance gave us a vision and put discipline into our lives. We had led scrambled lives with no sense of direction or destiny. His sincerity and ongoing interest in our future success has meant the most to us."

ED & JAN EVERITT — Musicians

"Michael has a unique ability to inspire others to seek and maintain a positive attitude"

GORDON LOWRY — Sales Mgr., Del Monte

"Michael's teaching was very enlightening and motivated me to return to the basics concerning success. It was well worth the time and money invested and I recommend him to anyone."

ANDY GENITI — Real Estate Broker

"Michael's teaching changed the way I think about my day to day activities. I now approach problems in a positive way. I also grew in discipline which enhanced every area of my life."

JIM PAINTER—Nursing Home Administrator

"Michael's teaching has greatly improved the attitude and productivity of my managers and department heads. The change in turn has affected the rest of personnel."

JOHN BORRESEN—Hotel GM

America's Battle for Free Enterprise

America's Battle for Free Enterprise

MICHAEL J. MUCCIO

America's Battle for Free Enterprise
ISBN: 978-1-936314-79-9
© 2012 by Michael J. Muccio

Published by:
White Stone Books
Lakeland, FLorida

Distributed by:
Word & Spirit Publishing
PO Box 701403
Tulsa, OK 74170

Table of Contents

Acknowledgements

I am very grateful to live in America, a country in which I can honestly identify my opinion with no fear of retribution by the government. I write this book out of my deep appreciation and love for my country. With all our faults, I'm proud to be an American! I'm very thankful to mom and dad, Dominic and Elaine Muccio who were such outstanding parents. Dad, as a veteran of WWII planted the earliest seeds of patriotism and love of country within me as he told me some of the war stories from WWII. Mom and dad have already passed away, far too young, but I believe they'd be proud of this book, a book that certainly has an imprint of what they deposited in my life. There are many more people that contributed their various views that subscribed to my love and respect for free-enterprise and the value of incentive and competition.

It was Zig Ziglar that inspired me and articulated what makes America such a great and outstanding country. He certainly didn't ignore the faults and emphasized the importance of identifying the problems for the purpose of motivating others to join with me in coming up with wise solutions. The late Jack Kemp was also an inspiration in the opportunities I had to meet with him and listen to his thoughts about free-enterprise. The various mayors I've had the privilege of meeting with and relating to certainly made their impression on my life. I can't even begin to name the hundreds of great men and woman who have contributed their nuggets of wisdom and insights into my life. The section would go on and on, but I assure you that each individual left their mark. You can clearly see in my notes how many people have inspired me with their books and speeches. Throughout this book, I've drawn from many wise men and woman down through history that have shaped my thinking in how to solve our current challenges in our America the Beautiful.

A special thanks goes out to my publisher and all the insight and wisdom they provided during this project. Keith was there all through the journey of bringing this book through all the necessary phases and details to get it out into the marketplace. I'm inclined to think I have the greatest publisher in the world!

My older brother Tom, older sister Linda and younger brother Greg have greatly contributed to my heritage and love for family. My ex-wife Karla blessed me with two enormous joys, my son Joshua and daughter Arielle. For years I've said that I want to be just like them when I grow up. As a dad, I could not be more proud of my two children! Plus, my son has demonstrated great taste and wisdom in his marriage to Lisa. Then, there's my first grandchild, Gia, who is undoubtedly the most intelligent, loving and beautiful baby on the planet.

Dedication

This book is dedicated not only to my son Joshua, daughter Arielle, daughter-in-law Lisa, and grandchild Gia, but to the entire younger generation of Americans.

I choose to believe that we, the older generation will pass a baton that represents a country that has paid down it's enormous debt and courageously tackled and solved the many other problems we are currently facing. It's our patriotic duty to leave them a country that is even better than how it was left to us.

Introduction

Obama Wins a Second Term

America has spoken and awarded a second term to President Obama. Nevertheless, the problems we're facing as a nation are far too time sensitive to take time to celebrate because your candidate won. It's also no time to sulk if your candidate lost. Our government needs to be watched like a hawk to make sure nothing will be done that will cause years of regret in the future. If we've learned anything, every single vote in the house and the senate matters. Every single decision coming out of the oval office matters.

There are some who are deceived into thinking that a democrat in the oval office automatically means we're doomed until the next election. After-all, isn't their philosophy to enlarge the federal government as much as possible? The problems are too serious to sit on our hands, complain and become passive until the next election. The wisdom and principles laid out in this book are no respecter of presidents. Apathy on our part as citizens is dangerous! Get educated about the problems and pay attention to what's going on. Know what is up for vote in the house or senate and stay ready to call, send emails and write your representative. If we as individuals don't stay involved continuously then we become victims to lobbyists that only care about their narrow issue. If their voice is the most plentiful and we are silent then guess who wins.

Great businesses begin with an outstanding vision that keeps all the employees focused on the mission and values to keep the company on course. Great nations are also built around an outstanding vision that is intended to keep politicians and leaders on course. America has the Declaration of Independence and the Constitution as its vision but unfortunately it does not carry the kind of respect or appreciation that the Founding Fathers paid such a heavy price to obtain. Why? What has happened to the attitude toward these documents? For some reason politicians and government leaders today have exalted their own discretionary ideas and ideals above the age-old principles of the rule of law that our founding documents represent.

The intent of the Founding Fathers happens to match the history of economically prosperous nations down through history. In other words, other nations have learned from America's values of free-enterprise, incentive and competition to build very successful economies. Imagine that! These values are currently supported when comparing South Korea to North Korea. Over 20 thousand individuals were polled in 20 nations and 61% said that free-enterprise is the best system on which to base the future of the world.[1] Interestingly, the highest vote for free-enterprise came from China at 74% while the lowest came from France at 36%.² Even Communist countries now recognize the clear value of free-enterprise, incentive and competition. Yet, in America there are 29% who chose not to tout the merits of free-enterprise and their voice has become far too prevalent in the very nation that has produced such amazing prosperity and generosity to needy nations around the world. Why? Simply because the 71% are not able to articulate persuasively enough the values of free-enterprise, incentive and competition. I have a passionate desire to empower the 71% and lead some of the 29% from their misinformation and their tendency to fall into the trap of snake oil salesman.

Chapter one supplies a litany of illustrations of the practical results of incentive presented in an easy to understand and simple manner. The second chapter focuses on President Reagan's passion for these principles at a time when America was in similar trouble to what we're facing today. The facts and stats don't lie and you'll come away knowing that we can do it again if we'll implore the same wisdom that he used. Chapter three focuses on the big picture of what has and hasn't worked in nations around the globe. You'll be inspired by the fact that these principles work wherever leaders value and persist with their proven track record.

The fourth chapter outlines the relatively unknown facts of who we actually owe the $16 trillion to. Chapter five simplifies the concept of the rule of law in laymen's terms and introduces the origin of the independent

Federal Reserve Bank. The sixth chapter compares when the Federal Reserve courageously stuck with rule of law policies during the Reagan years to its more discretionary approach today. Chapter 7 highlights the philosophy of the non-partisan Simpson & Bowles attempt at getting the deficit under control. Unfortunately, the president chose not to utilize the wisdom of the commission he established. The eighth chapter gives an interesting perspective to comparing public to private unions. Chapter nine tackles the challenge of not letting greed and dishonesty spoil long term business success and many future jobs. Doing business and life fairly, squarely, and by the rules will always be the best path to steady growth. Politically speaking, we are in desperate need of statesman over gazers of the latest poll.

The tenth chapter is a fair and balanced look at the state of America's education and how we measure up to the rest of the world. We'll look at what is and isn't working. In chapter eleven we'll address the infamous 47% that was so popular in the election. Each individual within the 47% has their own unique circumstances and there are wise steps that can be taken to advance each one. Chapter twelve identifies a brief history of how the federal government has swelled to an unmanageable size. There is built in competition between the states that ends up raising the standard of excellence for the entire country. Plus, it is far more practical to the citizens in each state when each governor pursues answers to the unique challenges he or she has to solve. The thirteenth chapter identifies the chief cause of poverty within nations. An innovative and inspirational story outlines how one amazing individual has taken on the challenge of many of the lowest income people on the planet. His idea has the potential to change the landscape of our current welfare system into a strategy that will actually work. In the midst of the serious unfairness issues that need our attention many educators are wasting time and money stirring up trouble on issues that cause intelligent people to shake their head in disbelief. The final chapter encourages us to waste no time in facing and solving the problems in our country. The American people are made of quality fabric and well able to pull together to do whatever it takes to restore us to many winning seasons in the decades ahead. It can be done but it's going to take an educated populace. It requires all hands on deck! Upon concluding the book you'll no longer be satisfied to just cite the problems within our government. From now on you'll be one of the conscientious citizens that will invest your time, talent, energy and involvement to do your part to solve the problem. It all begins with educating yourself about the magnitude of the problems and challenges we're facing.

"The more government takes in taxes, the less incentive people have to work. What coal miner or assembly-line worker jumps at the offer of overtime when he knows Uncle Sam is going to take 60 percent or more of his extra pay?"[I]
—Ronald Reagan

"A wise and frugal Government, which shall restrain men from injuring one another, shall leave them otherwise free to regulate their own pursuits of industry and improvement, and shall not take from the mouth of labor the bread it has earned. This is the sum of good government."[II]
—Thomas Jefferson

1
Incentive: What's in It for Me

There is an age-old sales pitch of persuading people that you can get something for nothing. The world is full of suckers who are easily taken in by soft, easy choices that promise much and may deliver for a while, but eventually they have to pay the piper. Naturally, some governments and some politicians play to the nature of their constituents' lower angels. People who are unaware of the history of governments who promise security by using class warfare to make their cases tend to get enthralled by such promises. If they can be guaranteed an income with no risk and minimal work, their lower angels will opt for such an easy out. However, there is a driving force that comes up out of the spirit of man that sees through the lazy philosophy that essentially originated under totalitarian tutoring.

There are always a remnant of people in the earth that are not duped by the promises of man and governments. The Founding Fathers of the U.S.A. were those types of individuals. They possessed a courage and a willingness to take a risk that drove them

THERE ARE ALWAYS A REMNANT OF PEOPLE IN THE EARTH THAT ARE NOT DUPED BY THE PROMISES OF MAN AND GOVERNMENTS.

to walk to the beat of a different drummer. Their hunger for freedom was far greater than their lower angels attraction to security, ease and comfort. These people don't recoil from work, and they have a strong sense of purpose. In fact, they're highly motivated by their work, rather than leisure or recreation. What motivates people to do their work with quality and excellence? What creates in people the appetite to work hard, work smart, and finish a job quickly?

One day I was looking out my window, and I noticed a sanitation technician (garbage man) that was hustling through his route with amazing speed. With a flurry of activity, he was running from one garbage can to the other rapidly picking each up and emptying it into the truck. He had to be operating under a wise leader who had given him an incentive to complete as many houses as possible in a given day. We are wired up in such a way that we thrive when given an incentive, and we degenerate when there is little or no incentive. The nature of man is such that he always asks himself, "What's in it for me?" Leaders can either capitalize on this internal drive and motivation, or they can ignore it at their own peril. Wise leaders would never rob a man or woman of the self-respect and dignity of feeling the satisfaction of the incentive or reward that follows quality work. Only a cruel and incompetent father would cripple his offspring by not teaching the incentive of work and completing a well-done task.

Wise and moral governments will set up systems that will automatically provide the incentive of work for those who were not adequately raised with the responsibility of work.

It was an afternoon in June 2004, and my son, Joshua, called me on the phone all excited about various speeches that Ronald Reagan had given. The media was playing a number of clips from speeches in numerous settings in honor of him after his death was announced to the country. Joshua was sixteen, and he caught the middle of a newscast talking about Reagan. "Dad, when did this guy live? Did you know much about him? I've never heard anything so powerful. We need more people like him," Joshua passionately reported to me. I began to shed tears as he went on and on about how excited he was about what he had heard. I realized that my son had never been exposed to Reagan's passion for America, freedom, free enterprise and his belief in a higher authority. I was also proud to know my son, who was a sophomore in high school, had enough sense to recognize the wisdom of Reagan's common sense and vision.

President Reagan had a way of communicating complex matters in an understandable way. He once read a letter from a student on his national radio show that beautifully articulated why the freedom of free enterprise worked better than socialism. The letter referred to a class experiment in which fifteen volunteers engaged in a push-up contest. The first round transpired in socialist style where each participant shared equally in the rewards. Thirty push-ups was the limit, and the full amount of push-ups was averaged among the group. Each person was awarded one piece of candy for every five push-ups that the group averaged. There were four students who managed to complete the maximum thirty push-ups, and all of them combined averaged 16.2, which earned each person three pieces of candy.

The experiment continued, this time utilizing a free enterprise, capitalist style in which each student was rewarded for his/her own performance. Under free enterprise, seven students completed the maximum thirty push-ups, and the average number was 21.2! Amazingly, this represented a 30 percent increase over the socialist style. The bulk of the fifteen students benefited by earning more candy, an average of four pieces each, while only a few students ended up with less.

The cry from proponents of socialism identified the free-enterprise style as unfair because some students were in better shape or stronger. Perhaps some of them had some sort of inherent weakness that hindered their performances. Was it fair for seven students to earn a reward of six pieces of candy while a few only earned one or two?

Nevertheless, the actual productivity of the entire group was 30 percent greater with free enterprise than it was with socialism. Most of the group was better off in their tangible reward, and the few who earned less had a new vision and incentive to work harder and strengthen their physical condition for the future.

Interestingly, what if each of the seven higher earners chose to give one of their pieces of candy to disabled students who did not have the wherewithal to complete even one push-up? What would be the likelihood of that happening when each student only received three pieces of candy?

You cannot help the poor by destroying the rich. You cannot strengthen the weak by weakening the strong. You cannot bring about prosperity by discouraging thrift. You cannot lift the wage earner up by pulling the wage payer down. You cannot further the brotherhood of man by inciting class hatred. You cannot build character and courage by taking away men's initiative and independence. You cannot help men permanently by doing for them, what they could and should do for themselves.[1]

You don't have to be a brain surgeon or rocket scientist to understand that the incentive to make more money, accomplish more success or receive some degree of recognition for a job

> You cannot help the poor by destroying the rich. You cannot strengthen the weak by weakening the strong – *Abraham Lincoln*

well done is the way human beings are wired. Most people want to earn more money. Nearly everyone wants to accomplish greater success. Others want to start new businesses. Most students have ambition to try out for sports teams or audition for parts in a musical or drama. Even asking a girl out on a date holds the incentive of the girl saying *yes*. However, anytime a risk is attempted, there is always the chance of failing. Part of the challenge of the chase is the inherent risk of failing. Failing, in and of itself, is an absolute necessity to make any kind of meaningful progress.

I tried out for little league baseball when I was eight, and I got cut. I tried out when I was nine and got cut again. Once again, I tried out at ten and was cut for the third straight year! I was a short, skinny, little runt who had a hard enough time lugging my papers around while delivering my paper route. In Maumee, Ohio, they had a system whereby the better players were drafted by little league coaches attending the tryouts. If you got cut, you were sent to the minors where you could at least play the game. The kids who were good enough for little league were given a full baseball uniform complete with the outer and inner sox, the pants, shirt and hat. They looked like big-league ballplayers! They got to play under the lights, with a grass infield, base paths of rich, dark dirt, nice bleachers for the fans, concession stands and umpires that were actually dressed like umpires. They got their name announced over the loudspeaker, and the results of the games were in the paper with pictures and everything.

Unfortunately, the minors, those of us who were crummy, were thrown a shirt and a hat. We were banned to the field where the infield was made of sandy dirt, and the outfield was full of weeds and gopher holes. There were no lights, no bleachers, no concession stands, no loudspeaker, no newspaper write-ups and the umpires were half-blind, old men in their street clothes. Even though I kept getting sent to the minors, I was improving from season to season. My final year in minor league I was the starting pitcher in the all-star game. The next year was pony league tryouts and there were no minor leagues for that age group. In fact, not even everyone that had been playing little league would be selected because there just weren't enough teams. Most minor league kids didn't even try-out because their chances of being selected were slim.

Guess what? I made a team! I finally got to play under the lights with a full uniform and all the other bells and whistles. The incentive of learning to be good at the game of baseball motivated me sufficiently until I ended up being voted the most valuable player of my high school team. I still get a satisfied smile when I think of the moment my name was called at the spring sports banquet and I walked to the platform to receive the certificate and observed the plaque that would be placed in the trophy case where it still sits today. You might ask: was the risk of failing and the journey of improving my skills worth it? Absolutely. To this day, when coaching a team in sports and business; I am the chief cheerleader of the guy or gal who has less natural ability or starts slow but has the guts to fail their way to success.

If the coaches that made the decision to cut me in little league would have selected me, even though I wasn't good enough; and if they had played me equally alongside the better players, they would have punished both the better players and me, the weaker player. There would have been no reward or payoff for the better players who had developed their skills, and I would have had no incentive to work harder and improve my ability. Isn't it wiser to have disciplined one person and provided the incentive to either get better or quit the game than to discipline an entire team for one person's ineffectiveness? The concept in business is called "creative destruction."

Joseph Schumpeter, an Austrian economist, coined the seemingly paradoxical term *creative destruction,* and economists have adopted it as a definition of the free market's messy way of delivering progress.[2] It's where the free market makes the determination of what businesses survive and which ones fail or "don't make the cut." For example, let's say a business with little or no market share creates a new mobile phone that more people start to buy than the previous leader in the marketplace. In a relatively short period of time, the previous market leader experiences the effects of creative destruction. This process of creative destruction is the essential fact about capitalism. Imagine that, when I finally made the pony league (the big time), I contributed to creative destruction. Some other youngster evidently hadn't continued to develop his skills and had taken his placement on a team for granted, and in the marketplace, a new player took his place.

Interestingly, before it was called *creative destruction,* even the Bible expressed strong feelings about people who do not use the money entrusted to them versus those who take initiative to use the money to grow whatever they started with. The spirit of the parable also carries the meaning of using your talents and gifts to bring about increase and success. The man rewards the individuals in the parable who courageously take a risk to grow what they start with, and he firmly rebukes the fearful individual who doesn't even try to get results. He actually takes away the amount the fearful individual starts with, and he gives it to the most productive person. The text says:

"It's also like a man going off on an extended trip. He called his servants together and delegated responsibilities. To one he gave five thousand dollars, to another two thousand, to a third one thousand, depending on their abilities. Then he left. Right off, the first servant went to work and doubled his master's investment. The second did the same. But the man with the single thousand dug a hole and carefully buried his master's money.

"After a long absence, the master of those three servants came back and settled up with them. The one given five thousand dollars showed him how he had doubled his investment. His master commended him: 'Good work! You did your job well. From now on be my partner.'

"The servant with the two thousand showed how he also had doubled his master's investment. His master commended him: 'Good work! You did your job well. From now on be my partner.'

"The servant given one thousand said, 'Master, I know you have high standards and hate careless ways, that you demand the best and make no allowances for error. I was afraid I might disappoint you, so I found a good hiding place and secured your money. Here it is, safe and sound down to the last cent.'

"The master was furious. 'That's a terrible way to live! It's criminal to live cautiously like that! If you knew I was after the best, why did you do less than the least? The least you could have done would have been to invest the sum with the bankers, where at least I would have gotten a little interest.

"'Take the thousand and give it to the one who risked the most. And get rid of this "play-it-safe" who won't go out on a limb. Throw him out into utter darkness.'"[3]

At first glance it might not seem loving until you look a little deeper and understand that biblical love is not counterfeit or co-dependent. Some people might call it *tough love.* Actually, it's just that the text highlights a love that believes in the greatness and the individual dignity within each person created.

My experience in the lesson of "creative destruction" in little league baseball provided valuable impetus later in my athletic career. When trying out for basketball in the eighth grade, I was once again cut. Having learned the value of persistence, I began to work on my basketball skills daily. My older brother, who was in college studying business (including some classes taught by Ken Blanchard), felt I was a good enough investment that he bought me a backyard basketball goal. We couldn't afford pavement, but I had an idea. There were many homes under construction, so I obtained permission from builders to collect their unused, leftover bricks in a wheelbarrow. I created a court with multicolored and differing styles of bricks. Later, when the bricks settled, there were a couple of spots that a few bricks settled differently and caused the ball to bounce wildly for any opposing competition. This gave me a distinct home-court advantage when playing one-on-one with any friends. My uncle, the electrician, put up a spotlight so I could play after it got dark.

In the ninth grade, I made the team; and by the time I was a junior, I was eleventh in district in scoring. More importantly, I logged all of those hours of hard work building the homemade brick court and persistently practicing on my own to develop the needed skills. It's hard to imagine doing that had I not learned the payoff and incentive of sticking with my baseball goal. The autobiographies of Lou Gehrig and Bob Cousy contributed to my incentive and motivation to be the best I could be in the two sports. These lessons paved the way to the entrepreneurial mindset that was cultivated within me. The incentive of the reward that follows hard work, risk-taking, and learning from others is in great need of resurgence in America.

Data from the U.S. Department of Commerce released on Sept. 13, 2012, indicated an accelerating collapse of startup job creation in recent years. The study concluded that entrepreneurship in the United States is in a dire state.

Job creation at newly formed firms has slipped to an all-time low. The number fell "from 10.8 per thousand during the George W. Bush administration . . . to 7.8 per thousand during the Obama administration."[4]

The power of the incentive to work was learned the hard way in the settling of America. The Plymouth Company settlement in Maine fizzled quickly. The Jamestown settlement came within a whisper of failing because there was no individual incentive in the early stages. The investors who sponsored the initiative were frustrated because they weren't seeing any profits. Their socialistic model included them owning all the land and using their elite officers to manage matters. No amount of strong-arming the settlers was motivating them to do anything more than the minimum amount of work when the rewards for their work had nothing to do with their productivity. Thankfully, before they all died off due to starvation or disease, they realized they had to give incentives. They gave each man a certain amount of land to work based on the size of his family. Not too amazingly, the settlement began to flourish. However, in other areas, the hierarchical elitist model was again attempted, both in Maryland and the Carolinas. Once again, it didn't work until they deeded up the land to the individuals who were actually working it. Think about that. Once they had an incentive and reason to go to work early and work until dusk, entire families pulled together as a team, and prosperity followed.[5]

Comparisons abound that compare free-enterprise/capitalism to either communism or socialism. Rich DeVoss, co-founder of Amway,™ compared the farmers in the former Soviet Union who worked their normal nine-to-five day during harvest with the American farmer who turned on the lights on his tractor and worked into the night. However, we have a problem when as my friend and mentor, Zig Ziglar writes:

According to the United States Chamber of Commerce and the Princeton Research Institute, 76% of our high school students do not believe a business needs a profit, and nearly 50% of them cannot give you even one advantage that capitalism has over socialism. Sixty-three percent of American high school students feel the Federal Government should own the banks, railroads, and steel companies. Sixty-two percent do not believe a worker should produce to the best of his ability, which is another form of dishonesty."[6]

Now, that's scary! What's in the history and government textbooks our National Education Association (NEA) have chosen to use? It appears that low science and math scores are not the only problem being produced by our educational system. Zig goes on to write:

These things are frightening, but don't blame the kids. It's our fault. We write the books, build the schools and pay the educators, and own the radio stations as well as the newspapers and magazines. It is up to us to teach our sons and daughters the advantages of the free enterprise system."[7]

Most of my life I've been self-employed, and I've always appreciated the fact that I can look myself in the mirror every morning and know that the board has just met concerning my incentive to succeed. In other words, I'm solely responsible for the amount of business effectiveness that's accomplished. Nevertheless, particularly when growing up, I've had the pleasure of working for effective bosses along with some really misguided bosses. It's always been difficult for me to imagine why some bosses, managers or business leaders would not establish clear-cut, obvious incentives among their employees. What are they thinking? From the office worker to shipping, every single person should have an incentive to balance quality with quickness. The higher-quality and faster worker should be able to make more money, period.

The lack of incentives is a key reason why public-sector government jobs have such high expenses and low productivity. *Reader's Digest,* December 1975, reported that in 1915 you could make a telephone call from New York to San Francisco for 20 dollars, or you could mail 1000 first-class letters between the two cities. In 1974, you could call from New York to San Francisco after 9:00 P.M. for 65 cents, or you could write five letters for the same price. So the government broke up the telephone company.[8] Businesses have the incentive to do as much as they can and keep the expenses as low as possible whereas the government just raises taxes. Creativity is maximized in the private sector of the business community.

How did my early failure in little-league baseball cultivate a lifelong lesson in understanding the significance of the power of incentive? Because I lacked natural ability, I worked out much harder and longer than other kids to hone my skills. I ended up being selected as the most-valuable player of my high school baseball team, which once again reinforces my gratitude for being cut over and over in little league. I would have never accomplished that had I not been cut and forced to either quit baseball or work harder than most other kids. I played a little college baseball just to see how far I could go in the sport. At least I erased all future regrets by trying. I went as far as my talent enabled me in college baseball, and I finally accepted that professional baseball was not my destiny.

Through my high school years, I had some great summer and weekend jobs in the hotel industry. A new hotel was built, and I applied every single day for over a week until John the general manager finally decided to hire me because I was so persistent. He gave me a title of "miscellaneous manager." He had me go in the bar and serve as a bar-back, washing glasses during happy hour. Studying the bartenders' every move, I learned how to replace them if they ever called in sick. Meanwhile, I continued college studying business. It was quite a classy nightclub with Las Vegas-style entertainment and attractive cocktail waitresses. Plus, it was right across the street from Six Flags Over Texas™ and just up the road from the stadium where the Texas Rangers played. The professional ballplayers for both teams would come in our nightclub after the games. If I couldn't make it to the pros, this seemed like the next best thing.

The general manager of the entire hotel, restaurant and nightclub took a liking to me. We were a company that was owned by Prudential Life™ that specialized in managing hotels for owners and investors. We were very successful taking properties that were unprofitable and turning them into money-makers. Sometimes the company would hire young people before they even finished college if they thought they had great potential. The bottom line is that the company took a risk with me and asked me to manage the nightclub. If Texas had not lowered the drinking age to eighteen, naturally they would not have been able to even take a risk with me. Why did they take such a risk with me? My dad and older brother were both stars in their business careers, and much of their wisdom flowed into me by osmosis. Delivering the Toledo Blade before we moved to Texas from ages 8-12 didn't hurt. Also, doing nearly every job in the hotel and restaurant industry from ages 14-18 improved my overall street smarts. I also had acquired some leadership experienced as a manager of a couple different departments in the hotel industry during those years.

Success came quickly as we established the best figures, including the lowest expenses, the highest percentage of profit and one of the fastest growing top-line revenues. Soon they sent me in for a couple of weeks to jump-start another property they had just taken over. I was on the fast track with the company and they wanted me to be incentivized to help instead of compete with other properties.

The budget when I took over didn't enable me to give the employees raises, so I had to get creative to come up with something that would be effective. Establishing incentives for my employees was a key component to our quick success. I had each cocktail waitress and bartender keep track of the amount of beverages they sold on their shifts, and I posted the results. There was an incentive to sell more because they were rewarded accordingly. The competition was fun, and it gave them the initiative to outdo their own previous high, along with outperforming a fellow employee. Suddenly, I had a dozen individual salesmen and women doing their very best to post the highest possible numbers, and our revenue skyrocketed.

Later, as I worked as a consultant, establishing incentives was one of the first things I implemented, and it always, all the time, worked. How can it not work? Some owners balked, and I had to give them my best sales pitch until they got on board. If they didn't get on board, I either didn't take the account or they didn't hire me. Either way, it was just as well because my motivational speeches only lasted so long, without the "teeth" to back them up.

Occasionally, I'd get the owner onboard about incentives and then have some goofball middle manager that whined about how it wouldn't work for his department. After seeding him with my thoughts, I'd suggest he go home and creatively come up with more ideas. That went over real big! Some would look at me like a startled squirrel. Nevertheless, I was sincere. Economics professor Steven E. Landsburg writes, "Incentives matter. The literature of economics contains tens of thousands of empirical studies verifying this proposition, and not one that convincingly refutes it."[9] Leaders have to come up with incentives that will motivate their employees if they're going to increase productivity.

Leaders, are you aware that, "According to H.M. Greenberg's psychological evaluation of over 180,000 people, nearly 80% reluctantly go to work every day"?[10] Naturally, we all have the responsibility to change our attitudes about our work and to look at what we're grateful about in a job, or we can quit. However, we as leaders can wisely put systems in place and create an atmosphere that increases the odds of more people getting on board with the vision. Leaders must always remember my mentor Zig Ziglar's philosophy, "You can have everything in life you want if you will just help enough other people get what they want."[11] Leaders must put themselves in their employees'

NEARLY 80% OF PEOPLE RELUCTANTLY GO TO WORK EVERY DAY

shoes if they plan on getting maximum results. Let's do it!

Every government job has to be supported by the taxes paid by private sector businesses and their employees. The government jobs don't have to wrestle with free-market competition that unleashes creative destruction and they don't have to find the cheapest, highest-quality, shortest distance between two points. If a million government jobs are lost and those million jobs turn into private sector jobs, the unemployment may still be 8 percent, but it will be a stronger and more lucrative 8 percent in the big scheme of things. One survey showed that "the rate of productivity per man hour in government is 39% below the average productivity level of the private sector."[12]

Dr. Mark J. Perry, professor of economics and finance at the University of Michigan, points out that the employer's costs per hour for state and local government is $39.83, whereas in the private sector it's $27.49. According to an analysis by *USA Today:*

> The number of federal employees making $100,000 or more has increased by 120,595, from 262,163 employees in December 2007 to 382,758 in June 2009, for a 46% increase. The number of federal workers making $150,000 or more has more than doubled since the recession started, from about 30,000 to more than 66,000. . . . When the recession started, the

Transportation Department had only one person earning a salary of $170,000 or more. Eighteen months later, 1,690 employees had salaries above $170,000. That's a 168,900% increase! The average unemployment from December 2007-2010 for government workers is 3% and private-sector workers are 7.9%. The private sector has faced a jobless rate more than twice as high as the rate for government workers over the last several years.[15]

The incentive to get ahead of competition in the free market creates lower expenses and higher quality as the strong survive and the weak die off. Interestingly, the losses are often only temporary because they regroup and start another business learning from their previous mistakes. They chip away at previous competitors, and the entire country is blessed as a result of the rugged struggle between free-market forces.

"Four years ago we said we would invigorate our economy by giving people greater freedom and incentives to take risks and letting them keep more of what they earned. We did what we promised and a great industrial giant is reborn."[I]
—RONALD REAGAN

"Competition is not only the basis of protection to the consumer, but is the incentive to progress."[II]
—HERBERT HOOVER

"The wise and correct course to follow in taxation and all other economic legislation is not to destroy those who have already secured success but to create conditions under which everyone will have a better chance to be successful."[III]
—CALVIN COOLIDGE

2
How the Gipper Got it Right— Reagan and Today

Ronald Reagan said, "No government ever voluntarily reduces itself in size. Government programs, once launched, never disappear. Actually, a government bureau is the nearest thing to eternal life we'll ever see on this earth!"[1] I bring up President Reagan because as Senator DeMint mentions, "Reagan slowed the growth of centralized federal power, lowered taxes, reduced regulations, and strengthened our military. His policies encouraged investment, innovation, and economic growth. The conservative Reagan Revolution spurred twenty years of economic growth."[2]

I remember those years from 1980 to 1988 quite well. Our nation was in very difficult times both economically and in matters of patriotism. The Cold War with the Soviet Union seemed to be going in their favor considering how much the defense had been cut by previous administrations. Reagan's philosophy of "peace through strength" along with turning the economy around were chief reasons for the crumbling of the Soviet Union and all its communist allies in eastern Europe. Many other positive results came from the rebuilding of our military, with one example being the invasion of Grenada.

Although criticized by the media and the United Nations, the people of Grenada were thrilled enough to make the date of the invasion a national holiday which they call "Thanksgiving."

A *Wall Street Journal* article points out:

When Mr. Reagan took office in January 1981, inflation was running at roughly a 12% rate, compared to the 3% or so that's likely holding sway now. Mortgage interest rates were staggering, having topped 16%. Unemployment was at 7.5%, and on its way to 10.8%. Oil prices were triple what they had been four years earlier. Though nobody knew for sure then, the economy was heading into a long and hard recession in the latter half of 1981 and into 1982 . . . . Reagan entered office saying . . . that government was the problem. Today, with the Federal Reserve having just about run out of monetary options to stimulate the economy, almost everybody believes the government, through stimulative spending and tax-cutting policies, has to be a big part of the solution.[3]

President Reagan's rule-of-law, free-market approach gave him the strength of character to endure the recession of his first two years, not by looking for the government to bail out the challenges but by creating an atmosphere for the free market to do what only free enterprise can do. He used the pulpit of the presidency to inspire the kind of subjects that cultivated patriotism and a positive attitude. It was a combination of the "right policies" and wise, visionary leadership that inspired the country and made us proud to be Americans again. He had written a book entitled *Abortion and the Conscience of the Nation* and gave speeches on the oddity of removing prayer from school in 1962. In his February 25 radio address he commented:

> Sometimes I can't help but feel the first amendment is being turned on its head. Because ask yourselves: can it really be true that the first amendment can permit Nazis and Ku Klux Klansmen to march on public property, advocate the extermination of people of the Jewish faith and the subjugation of blacks, while the same amendment forbids our children from saying a prayer in school? . . . Teddy Roosevelt told us, "The American people are slow to wrath, but when their wrath is once kindled it burns like a consuming flame." Up to 80 percent of the American people support voluntary prayer. They understand what the Founding Fathers intended. The first amendment of the Constitution was not written to protect the people from religion; that amendment was written to protect religion from government tyranny. The amendment says, "Congress shall make no law respecting an

establishment of religion or prohibiting the free exercise thereof." What could be more clear?[4]

Invariably, Reagan's critics point out how much he increased the debt. I've heard numerous news interviews that say by every measure he increased the debt more than any other president. It is commonly communicated that Reagan actually increased the debt more than it has been increased in the last four years. I remember the challenges that he faced in those years with House Speaker Tip O'Neill, and how Reagan's balanced budgets never left the House of Representatives "balanced." Reagan felt strongly about it and said, "It (a balanced-budget amendment) must prevail because if it does not, the free society we have known for two hundred years, the ideal of a government by consent of the governed, will simply cease to exist."[5]

I decided to evaluate the findings and analyze the conclusions of those who criticized Reagan. I went to numerous sources to acquire the actual numbers. This way I was able to simplify and explain the calculations of all the numbers in an understandable manner. First off, indeed the debt has been slowly climbing since World War II. Upon studying the numbers, I discovered that the TV "talking heads" I heard were leaving out the very important comparison of the debt to GDP.

To understand the comparison, imagine that the country adds $1 billion in debt while at the same time earning only $1 billion. That would be a 100-percent debt-to-earnings rate (GDP). Instead, let's say the country earned $2 billion to offset the $1 billion in debt. That would be a 50-percent rate of debt to GDP. You always have to look at the rate of debt to what the free market is earning or you'll miss the point as to why America's debt is far more serious now than at any other time—other than immediately after World War II, except that now the actual numbers are so huge. Another way to consider the matter is the importance of a business increasing its top line of revenue, not just its bottom line. For example, if a business earns $1 million in revenue and its expenses are 80 percent or $800 thousand, it has made a $200 thousand profit. Then if it makes that $1 million in revenue every year for the next ten years with the same expenses, there won't be many investors flocking to buy stock in a company that's not showing any growth. If, on the other hand, a business increases its revenue by 10 percent a year over the next ten years while maintaining its expenses at the same 80-percent rate, then investors will be thrilled to invest in a company that's showing such steady growth. Let's say a business borrows $1 million and then turns it into increased revenue of $800 thousand over the next eight years. Naturally, that is a wise loan. Granted, there are not very many people in politics who have built successful businesses, and herein lies the problem. There is a big difference in borrowing money to take a calculated business risk in hopes of increasing revenue and profit margin versus borrowing money to pay ongoing operational expenses to survive. A wise businessman will cut expenses because he knows that borrowed money must be used to take a calculated risk that will potentially increase revenue.

Let's compare the mathematics of President Reagan's accomplishments to our current challenges. First, let's look at the last time in our history that our debt was over 100 percent of GDP. At the end of World War II in 1945, GDP (Gross Domestic Product, our annual national earnings) was $223 billion while the national debt was $259 billion, 116 percent of GDP.[6] Naturally, it was the cost of World War II and the loss of productivity due to so much of the populace being abroad and fighting in the war. When studying the numbers, there has been a steady climb in the percent of debt to GDP since World War II that every president has added to the pot. However, keep in mind that Congress is even more of a culprit to adding to the debt than presidents.

REAGAN ESSENTIALLY USED FREE-ENTERPRISE/ CAPITALISM TO BANKRUPT A COMMUNIST SYSTEM.

When President Reagan was sworn in, the debt was 33.3 percent of GDP, and the GDP was $2.78 trillion. The actual debt was $930 billion. One of the ways the previous administration tried to tackle the weak economy was by making steep cuts in military expenditures. Reagan felt this was dangerous due to the threat of the large military build up of the Soviet Union, so he promised to rebuild defense and lower taxes to stimulate the economy. In Reagan's last year, the debt was 52.6 percent of GDP, and the actual GDP was $5.1 trillion. The actual debt was $2.68 trillion. In other words, coming out of a bad recession, Reagan created an atmosphere between government and business that caused GDP to increase a colossal 82 percent! This happened even though in order to fulfill his plan he had to make deals and negotiate with the other party that controlled the House of Representatives.[7] For example, Reagan's strategic defense initiative caused the Soviets to spend up to 35 percent of GDP to match Reagan's use of 15-18 percent of GDP on defense.[8] Naturally, free-enterprise America was strong enough to endure that kind of spending, but the Communist Soviet Union was brought to its knees without a shot ever having to be fired, thus, "peace through strength." Reagan essentially used free-enterprise/capitalism to bankrupt a communist system he called "the evil empire." Reagan's approach had set the stage for the eventual collapse of communism in 1991.

Let's compare the current economic woes to what Reagan faced and see how our numbers are faring today. In 2008, the debt was 74.1 percent of GDP, which was $14.44 trillion. The actual debt was $10.69 trillion. In 2009, the debt grew to 86.4 percent of GDP, while the GDP actually decreased to $14.26 trillion, which is rare. The actual debt was $12.31 trillion. In 2010, the debt grew to 95.1 percent of GDP, which was $14.74 trillion. The actual debt was $14.02 trillion. In 2011, the debt reached 98.7% of GDP, which was $15.32 trillion. The actual debt was $15.12. In mid-2012, the debt was 101.7 percent of GDP, which was $15.59 trillion.[9] The actual debt in October of 2012 was already over $16.21 trillion and rising. This means the United States debt is larger than what the country is actually producing in GDP. The debt has increased in the last four years by 27.6 percent of GDP, while the actual GDP increased only 3-4 percent. Reagan increased the debt in his administration, but the GDP could substantiate the increase. Once again, Reagan increased the debt in his eight years by 18.4 percent of GDP, but he also dramatically increased the GDP by 82 percent. Today, the increased debt is not being offset by an adequate increase in GDP. Could it be the difference between depending on the government to solve our economic woes instead of Reagan's philosophy of a bigger government actually being the problem? Thus, he shrunk the government as best he could while negotiating with members of the other party, along with building up the defense.

Someone might say that in order to be fair, we should compare Reagan's first four years to the United States' most recent, last four years:

Debt	GDP	percent to GDP
1980 - $930 billion	$2.78 trillion	33.3%
1981 - $1.02 trillion	$3.13 trillion	32.9%
1982 - $1.19 trillion	$3.25 trillion	36.8%
1983 - $1.41 trillion	$3.53 trillion	39.9%
1984 - $1.66 trillion	$3.93 trillion	42.3%

Reagan increased the percent of debt-to-GDP by 9 percent from 33.3 percent in 1980 to 42.3 percent in 1984. The percent of debt-to-GDP was increased by 28.9 percent from 74.1 percent in 2008 to 101.7 percent in 2012.[10] Actual dollar-amount size of the GDP increase during the Reagan years is nearly as great as the last four years, which is quite phenomenal when you think about it. The consumer-price index indicates that the actual buying power in 1984 is over twice the amount of what it is in 2012. In fact, it's exactly 121.7 percent greater.[11] The actual dollar amount of GDP increase in Reagan's first term from 1980 to 1984 was $1,143,700,000,000. The GDP increase from 2008 to mid-2012 is $1,153,600,000,000. An increase in GDP of $1.14 trillion from 1980 to 1984 is twice as meaningful as the increase in today's buying power of a relatively meager $1.15 trillion from 2008 to mid-2012. Whatever was done in the Reagan years to accomplish that kind of growth should be studied and learned in every college around the world. The mathematics don't lie. Said in another way, in Reagan's first four years, the GDP increased 41 percent, while from 2008 to 2012 the GDP only increased 8 percent.

FREE ENTERPRISE/ CAPITALISM IS THE KEY TO OUR NATIONS FUTURE ECONOMIC PROSPERITY.

There is a great need in the United States for political leaders that are visionaries who understand and are able to articulate sensible business principles to a populace that doesn't fully grasp why free-enterprise/capitalism is the key to our nation's future economic prosperity. Far too many people look to the government to co-dependently "rescue" and "take care" of the problems we face as a nation. In so many ways, we come across as a nanny state. Reagan said, "Socialists ignore the side of man that is the spirit. They can provide you shelter, fill your belly with bacon and beans, treat you when you're ill, all the things guaranteed to a prisoner or a slave. They don't understand that we also dream."[12] Abraham Lincoln said, "America will never be destroyed from outside. If we falter and lose our freedoms, it will be because we destroyed ourselves."[13]

*"Socialism is a philosophy of failure,
the creed of ignorance, and the gospel of envy."*[i]
—WINSTON CHURCHILL

*"The great dialectic in our time is not,
as anciently and by some still supposed,
between capital and labor; it is between
economic enterprise and the state."*[ii]
—JOHN KENNETH GALBRAITH

*"Socialists cry 'Power to the people,'
and raise the clenched fist as they say it.
We all know what they really mean—
power over people, power to the State."*[iii]
—MARGARET THATCHER

3

How to Screw up a Nation in One Easy Lesson

Why do some nations succeed financially while others do not? Although aware of the reason, I still wanted an up-to-date analysis of the subject. I contacted college professors, librarians, and others that I thought could steer me toward a thorough and well-documented study or book. This quest continued for a couple of months while I was writing another book. Then one day, I ran into a book being promoted that was scheduled to be released in three or four months called, *Why Nations Fail.* Perfect! I preordered the book written by Daron Acemoglu, an award-winning economist and MIT professor, and James A. Robinson, a political scientist, economist, and professor at Harvard. A key component is that countries differ because of their varying institutions, the various rules influencing how the economy works and the incentives that motivate people.

The authors ask the reader to imagine teenagers in North and South Korea and what they might expect from life. Those in the North grow up without incentives or adequate education to prepare them to start a business. In fact, there are few books and computers and much of their education is propaganda to strengthen the hold of the communist regime. Once they complete their brainwashing, they go into the army for ten years. They will not be able to own property, have legal access to markets, or grow more prosperous.

Meanwhile, those in the South grow up with incentives that encourage them to exert effort and excel. They're motivated to someday own their own property, learn the marketplace, start their own business, and prosper in every way they can imagine. There is a reason and motivation to work hard, so they can buy what they want for their families. It's the same spirit that exists in the United States, whereas North Korea parallels Castro's Cuba. They write, "A businessman who expects his output to be stolen, expropriated, or entirely taxed away will have little incentive to work, let alone any incentive to undertake investments and innovations."[1] A country that has political institutions that concentrate power in the hands of a narrow elite will never utilize the creative power of the citizens. Instead, the elites devise institutions that control and extract resources from the rest of society. The elites proceed to pick their favorites that will fully cooperate with their agenda. The idea of the free market competing with one another yields to the elite's preferential treatment.

Free enterprise institutions pave the road for creative entrepreneurs like Thomas Edison, R.G. Letourneau, David Green, Bill Gates, Steve Jobs,

Sergey Brin, Larry Page, Jeff Bezos, and Mark Zuckerberg. Is it any surprise that the USA produced these type of individuals and not "Mexico or Peru . . . and that it was South Korea, not North Korea, that today produces technology innovative companies such as Samsung and Hyundai"?[2] This kind of talent will continue to be birthed in free-enterprise countries because teenagers in the United States can get as much schooling as they choose to capitalize on. The authors identify examples in history where countries restricted their prosperity by their institutions.

The economic crisis in Europe is highlighting the lack of incentive in countries that are leaning more socialistic than waving the banner of free-enterprise/capitalism. Canadian Mark Steyn writes:

> Greek public servants have their nose to the grindstone 24/7. They work twenty-four hours a week for seven months of the year. It's not just that every year you receive fourteen monthly payments, but that you only do about thirty weeks' work for it. For many public-sector "workers," the work day ends at 2:30 P.M. Gosh, when you retire on your fourteen monthly pension payments, you scarcely notice the difference, except for a few freed-up mornings. Couldn't happen in America, right?"[3]

Reuters reported that "Washington, D.C., has become the favorite area for wealthy young adults, with the nation's highest percentage of 25-34 year-olds making more than $100,000 a year."[4] Is it true that the easiest way to a "lifestyle" is a government job? *Newsweek* did a survey and found that "seven of the ten wealthiest counties in the United States were in the Washington commuter belt."[5] What is that saying about the direction our country is moving? Where is wealth creation occurring in proximity to industry or government? Ouch!

Countries around the globe are currently suffering because of a breach in integrity and honesty among leaders and at the grassroots level of the culture. The idea of being pure, genuine, sincere and honest through and through is treated like naive foolishness. Is it common or uncommon for many people to naturally revert to telling half-truths, misleading or outright lying? This tends to make encounters with people somewhat of a toss-up. We have to ask ourselves is this person shooting straight with me? Is it a half-truth, or is it a bald-faced lie?

A PERSON WHO LACKS THE COURAGE TO SAY NO, IN DUE TIME, THEIR YESES WILL BE MEANINGLESS.

Nothing sucks the life out of a prosperous nation and economy more than dishonesty. If people in authority can't be trusted to actually tell the truth, then the entire fabric of our society rots from within. If a politician says whatever is necessary to get elected and then continually projects himself as all things to all men, his lack of courage and deceitfulness is destructive to the very people who voted him into power. A person who lacks the courage to say no, in due time, their yeses will be meaningless. Wise leadership requires priorities, which creates decisiveness and action when those who are politically correct are frozen by fear and procrastination. A lack of taking an authentic and honest stand for truth and what is right will continually cause a leader to pander to the lower angels of human nature.

Honesty starts with me. Can I be trusted to tell the truth? Once I'm at least quickly recognizing any half-truths that slip out of my own mouth and acknowledging those errors of judgment as they occur, then I contribute to raising the honesty level of the entire planet. That's how easy each of us can increase the chances of hearing the truth from politicians, lobbyists, government officials, business owners, educators, attorneys, judges and media. Make no mistake; it all starts with each of us as individuals on the grassroots level. I realize that there will always be people with a seared conscience who can look you in the eye and tell a bald-faced lie. However, once you are on the honesty road, you will be less inclined to be deceived by liars. You'll tend to just know on the inside and intuitively separate truth from falsehood.

One of the great coaches I respected was the late Vince Lombardi who said, "It is a reality of life that men are competitive and the most competitive games draw the most competitive men. That's why they are there—to compete. To know the rules and the objective when they get in the game. The object is to win fairly, squarely, by the rules—but to win." We all respect and value those who compete and win. Yet, we are disgusted with those who resort to cheating and dishonoring the game by not competing fairly, squarely and by the rules. Whether it's an athlete turning to performance-enhancing drugs, or football players being offered a bounty to hit their opponents with the purpose of injuring them, the lack of integrity is grieving. Perhaps I'm naive and what came to light with one NFL team happens more often than I, as a fan, realize. All players are not "Saints"! However, I find it hard to believe that a true athlete with any self-respect and dignity would actually try to physically injure or maim an opponent. I choose to believe that nearly every honest athlete would cringe at the thought of running the risk of hurting someone for life because they did not play the game fairly, squarely and by the rules.

For example, I had an interesting experience in one of my senior-year, high-school football practices. I was playing tight end, and we were running the opposing team's plays to prepare our first-team defense for what they would be facing on Friday night. Evidently, the team we were playing used a quick pass to the tight end with a great deal of success. Interestingly, our defensive coach was over with us on the offense, calling the plays, and purposely trying to trip up his defense. We took our football serious in Texas! I particularly enjoyed our fifty-two quick pass because, with our wishbone offense, it was about the only time as a tight end I got to touch the ball. As a basketball player, I had lots of opportunities to regularly touch the ball. That's why I was a catcher in baseball; I got to handle the ball on every play. Anyway, I had caught several quick passes against the defense for nice gains, and the head coach finally had had enough and got really ticked off at his defense. He yelled out, "Run it again!" Immediately, I thought, *Well, crap, now they know it's coming.* We had been mixing it in with other plays. I registered my complaint in the huddle to the coach, and he played the quarterback position on the next play and gave me a slight way to alter the route. The particular defender responsible for covering me loved to hit hard and make you remember it. He used to play full-back, but he kept going out of his way to find some-body to run over instead trying to avoid the defense and focus on getting yardage. It made sense to move him to defense.

That was all good and fine, but now he knew it was coming. Nevertheless, I altered the route but stayed within the boundaries of the quick pass and caught it again, but this time I got hit by the defender pretty quick and hard for a smaller gain. The head coach yelled out, "Run it again!" Back in the huddle, the defensive coach agreed to throw it really quick, and he took the quarterback position again. I caught it again, but this time the defender hit me hard and low, woefully close to my knees, and my temper kicked in. I threw the ball at him and he ripped his helmet off ready to fight. I figured I'd leave my helmet on, I thought it might come in handy in a fight. After all, it was a practice: what's the point of grandstanding? There were no fans. Either way, the coaches and players quickly broke us up. I realized he was just doing his job, but he came too close to my knees for comfort. I highly valued my knees. My senior year in baseball was coming up, and as a catcher, my knees were quite important. I don't really think the defender was trying to hurt me, but in the heat of the moment, I lost it. We made up in the locker room, and all was fine.

What's my point? In football, it's not that difficult to badly injure an opponent if that's your intention. In marketing a product, it's easy enough to lie if that's your intention. In running for political office, it's easy enough to lie about your opponent and take one of their comments out of context if that's your intention. In business, it's easy enough to lie to your stockholders if that's your intention. If you're in the media, it's easy enough to smear someone by taking one phrase out of a twenty-minute speech or interview to build your misleading case. If you have no trepidation of the law of sowing and reaping, or as some identify it as negative karma, then why be the least bit uneasy about being dishonest and freely lying? Some people have the concept backwards; they lie like there is a reward for it.

Zig Ziglar writes, "Dr. Mortimer Feinberg, author of *Corporate Bigamy,* interviewed one hundred top executives with Fortune 500 companies. These men said that anyone who thinks he can get to the top and stay there without honesty is dumb. That's strong, and it's accurate."[6] The famous Harvard Professor and psychiatrist, Dr. Robert Coles, was interviewed by David Gergen. He said:

> I'm trying to insist . . . as a parent and a teacher and for all of us, that we remember that any lesson offered a child in (the) abstract . . . is not going to work very well. We live out what we presumably want taught to our children. And our children are taking constant notice, and they're measuring us not by what we say but what we do.

He went on to point out the importance of teaching about character and morals both at home and at schools, and he commented,

> But it's interesting how little attention is paid in our schools and universities, never mind in our public discussions to this aspect of life, mainly character and moral development, meaning moral living as children learn it, at home and in school. For instance, Harvard University and some of the other universities where some of

us teach were originally founded for the instal-
lation of character, if you read the early charter
that got these schools going.

Gergen asked about the importance of stories, and
Dr. Coles responded,

Stories are—we know from the Bible—they're
the way to teach. Stories encourage the moral
imagination to work, and they are concrete and
connected to everyday experience.

Gergen said:

It's interesting to me that you spoke frequently
in your book about the moral loneliness of children; they sometimes feel morally abandoned;
that they really do need a moral guidance. You
said, children very much need a sense of
purpose and direction on life, a set of values
grounded in moral introspection; a spiritual life
that is given sanction by their parents and
others in the adult world.

Coles answered:

They all ask these endless whys, and these are
not to be dismissed as merely going through a
psychological stage. These whys are affirming
their humanity, and these whys show their moral
hunger, and we ought to figure out even as we're

wondering about how we're going to feed them correctly with the right amount of vitamins, we ought to be thinking about these moral aspects of their hunger, and try to figure out how to feed that, and by the way, feed ourselves.[7]

It is amazing as a child how much you watch adults and do what they do. I've mentioned previously that I delivered a paper route. It was a walking route in which I delivered the paper between the external storm or screen door and the wooden door. Many of my customers would see me coming and come to me to get their papers and walk down the street reading it. Others would meet me at the front and start reading the paper before they even closed the front door. In my young mind, I assumed that the *Toledo Blade* newspaper was really important, so I would also read it as I was walking from house to house. I remember how confusing it was to learn from the newspaper that there was such a thing as dishonest congressmen, senators and presidents. As a little boy, mom or dad had told me about George Washington saying when asked who chopped down the cherry tree, "I cannot tell a lie. I chopped down the cherry tree." From that point forward, I determined to never chop down a cherry tree. I'm happy to say that in my entire wild life, I have never once chopped down a cherry tree.

Back to the politicians, I did understand the moral of the story about young George; and in my mind, I'd just assumed that it was a prerequisite for politicians to be honest. In reading those papers I was delivering, I noticed the various headlines about all manner of lying and dishonesty within various government officials. It scared me because most of the money I saw had honest George's face on it, and I figured if these guys were lying, what was going to happen to the country? Didn't they know about our first president? Didn't they know lying was wrong? In case you don't know, delivering papers in the 1960s introduced me to a smorgasbord of negativity, and much revolved around some form of dishonesty.

I love my country! Dad and I watched war movies, and every Tuesday night at 7:30, the TV series, *Combat* would come on. Dad would tell me the World War II stories of how America helped Europe maintain freedom by stopping Hitler and Mussolini and then turning attention to the Pacific to stop Emperor Hirohito and his Prime Minister Tojo. I am proud to be an American. Why were important people in our government lying? I remember watching reruns of the movie, *Mr. Smith Goes to Washington,* with Jimmy Stewart, which had been an immediate hit, second only to *Gone with the Wind* in 1939 box-office receipts. The movie portrayed the dishonesty among politicians and businessmen that I was reading about. Lobbyists connived on behalf of a

HONESTY STARTS BY THE GOVERNMENT FOLLOWING THE SAME RULES CONCERNING IT'S EXPENSES AS ANY FAMILY OR PRIVATE SECTOR BUSINESS OR ORGANIZATION.

business, union or special interest to control and get their way with congressmen and senators. The politicians actually deceitfully passed bills that weren't really in the very best interest of the country. What was going on in America the Beautiful?

Fast-forward to today. Honesty starts by governments following the same rules concerning its expenses as any family or private-sector business or organization. A business or family cannot automatically raise its budget when the income is not there to support it. However, a government can actually raise expenditures even when the income is not balancing out such a decision. A business or family can't raise taxes or print money to get out of the problem. A loan would have to be approved by the lender, and that very step runs the risk of hurting the business or family in the future. Printing money for families and businesses is, of course, dishonest, and jail is offered as quite a deterrent! When our government's income is down due to less revenue from the people who pay taxes, then governments must cut their expenses just like families and businesses. If they don't, then they cause a greater loss of revenue in the future. Putting off today's painful and courageous choice blocks the release of the problem-solving incentive for the private sector to find new and creative solutions.

A COURAGEOUS STATESMAN RULED BY INTEGRITY WILL DO THE RIGHT THING EVEN IF IT MIGHT COST HIS JOB.

Remember honest George Washington referred to earlier? He said, "I hope I shall always possess firmness and virtue enough to maintain what I consider the most enviable of all titles, the character of an 'Honest Man.'"[8] Is it honest and truthful if an elected official makes a decision for the purpose of satisfying a lobbyist who has bought his or her favor? Is it honest if he or she operates in a manner to get re-elected without considering what is best for both his or her district and the overall country? A courageous statesman ruled by integrity will do the right thing even if it might cost his job. We surely need more statesmen in our government like Mr. Smith played by Jimmy Stewart.

Life will become much simpler when truth, honesty and doing the right thing is at the core of those involved in making the decisions. Winston Churchill said, "A vocabulary of truth and simplicity will be of service throughout your life."[9] What are "we the people" going to do? The only option for the so-called "ignorant masses," in other words, you and me, is to educate us to dig deeper and to stop being duped by lies and half-truths. Let's all sift through and reveal the nonsense and dishonesty. Niccolo Machiavelli said, "One who deceives will always find those who allow themselves to be deceived."[10] Once again, honesty starts at the grassroots level with each one of us. We must choose honesty and integrity as how we're going to win, "fairly, squarely, by the rules." The ignorant masses can introduce change with society by raising the bar and contributing to honesty dominating the landscape of our country. William Shakespeare wrote, "Ay, sir; to be honest, as this world goes, is to be one man picked out of ten thousand."[11]

Concerning dishonesty, oftentimes people will say, "Well everybody else is doing it. Therefore, I have to act the same way in order to compete." In other words, to beat the other guy, "I have to lie like everyone else." Wow! What an exciting incentive to rule your life by. That vision will excite you to get out of bed every morning. As you say to yourself, "Oh boy, I'm going to fit into the mold of everybody else on the planet that has justified the habit of lying." Doesn't that vision inspire you to be a wonderful example to your children, your mate, and your co-workers? Tamar Frankl, author of *Trust and Honesty: America's Business Culture at a Crossroads*, writes:

> Make no mistake about it. America will continue to have its con artists, rogue brokers, and powerful white-collar abusers to trust. That will not change. What should change are the general attitude and the tolerance of dishonesty. What should change is the direction of America's culture to an aspiration to honesty, an aspiration that "goes without saying." Attitude and aspiration redirect and transform culture.[12]

The incentive to develop a habit of telling the truth and resisting the temptation to lie is huge. You can temporarily fool people for a season, but the price to pay when the lights go out and it's just you and your own thoughts is something worth considering. Doesn't that loom larger than any temporary gain? Plus, according to the studies already mentioned, the loss of effective long-term influence far outweighs any temporary benefit. What's the point of risking your future by doing to someone else the opposite of what you would want done to you? Life is far too short to plant negative seeds that will boomerang back at you.

Dr. Steven Berglas writes:

Most folks know who is responsible for the observation, "If you tell a big enough lie and tell it frequently enough, it will be believed." It was Hitler. Now I am not saying all tellers of Big Lies should be lumped with Hitler, but it is undeniable that our nation is now awash with politicians repeating lie after lie, ad nauseam, and those doing it believe we will buy into it. What may be worse than this fact is that few among us are bristling with righteous indignation about being treated so contemptuously. I, for one, am infuriated not just because folks are insulting my intelligence, but because, as an advocate for all matters related to entrepreneurship, the lies coming out of Washington, D.C. make it virtually impossible for my constituency to do their thing. . . . The thing is, what liars are not aware of is that using deceit to "make it" in America is the easy part. It's staying on top that is hard, and enjoying one's success, long-term, is hardest of all. . . . Every successful person I know who used lies to make it suffered psychologically for years after his headlines had faded. Which is why I am so adamant about advising that you should never lie to advance professionally. . . . If you advocate a position you know is false, your body picks up on the conflict—however minor—your mind is sensing. This negative effect then shoots a bunch of hormones into your system . . . that, if not utilized to address a physical danger, build up over time and cause damage to your circulatory system (heart, veins, arteries) and major organ systems. When you are honest, not only are stress-fighting hormones withheld, your body emits "happy hormones" . . . that actually enhance your good mood. . . . George Bernard Shaw . . . gets the Blue Ribbon for the most insightful justification for being 100% truthful 100% of the time. As he put it: "The liar's punishment is not in the least that he is not believed, but that he cannot believe anyone else."[13]

None of us should ever slip into over-confidence or, worse yet, cockiness, concerning the crucial choices of everyday life. We're all subject to the temptations of being deceived at any given moment. Let's at least recognize that honesty and integrity is a worthy cause worth pursuing every single day and night the rest of our lives.

"I could end the deficit in 5 minutes.
You just pass a law that says that anytime
there is a deficit of more than 3% of GDP all sitting
members of congress are ineligible for reelection."[I]
—WARREN BUFFET

"We contend that for a nation to tax itself into
prosperity is like a man standing in a bucket
and trying to lift himself up by the handle."[II]
—WINSTON CHURCHILL

"The American Republic will endure until
the day Congress discovers that it can
bribe the public with the public's money."[III]
—ALEXIS DE TOCQUEVILLE

4

The Borrower Is Servant to the Lender

Before getting too far into this section, it seems wise to mention my concern about the two-party system of democrats and republicans. It's easy to understand why George Washington expressed such sober warnings of the two-party system in his farewell address. In his eight years in office, he chose to not give his allegiance to any one political party, referring to it as "the baneful effects of the spirit of party."[1] He saw a two-party system as a "frightful despotism."[2] Benjamin Franklin wrote that it would engender confusion. James Madison, Alexander Hamilton and John Jay, saw it as creating a "spirit of faction."[3] Obviously, we need honest statesmen in both parties that really understand business, economics, and free-enterprise/capitalism. There are already some great men and women in all branches of the government that are trying to get our attention at the grassroots level to elect more who are like-minded as they are.

For America to remain free, it is incumbent upon each of us to educate ourselves on the actual issues in a non-partisan way. We must carefully examine the actual voting record of current politicians to know exactly where they stand. We can no longer afford to just believe in their speeches and rhetoric. Far too often we've become a victim to sound bites and slogans that sound good but fall woefully short in sound mathematics. Let's smarten up and stop swallowing pie-in-the-sky promises that cannot possibly be fulfilled. If a new person is running for office, we need to hone in on the soundness of the economics, philosophy and principles that they propose to govern under. Depending on the circumstances and principles at stake, I've served both democrats and republicans. There is too much at stake to wait around for "Mr./Mrs. Right" to get elected. Once in office, we must evaluate each of their decisions with a fine-tooth comb.

It was my pleasure to honor the office of mayor and the democrat that held that post in our city. A relationship of genuine respect and concern was forged between us. At a point in time, he asked me to serve on a special commission concerning an issue that he felt was quite important to the city. The commission's job was to study the matter and make our recommendation to the mayor and city council. I remember complaining in one of our one-on-one meetings because the commission was so strongly moving away from the position I thought was best. He let me go on for a few minutes and then leaned forward in his chair and said, "That's why I put you on the commission, to express your view." He was kind in his mild reproof, but I left his office that day with my tail between my legs, determined to return to my office and write a thorough research paper citing the supporting evidence for my point. For two weeks, I spent my leisure and extracurricular time reading dozens of articles, studies, and books to compile the paper. I called the chairman to request twenty minutes on the agenda, and the next meeting I passed a copy of the paper out to everyone and read it aloud. Initially, you could have heard a pin drop after the paper was verbalized. There were many questions, and it triggered quite a debate. When the discussion was completed, over 80 percent shared the view that my research provided. The mayor was so impressed with the thoroughness of the research that he said he was going to send a copy to President Clinton. The only negative was when the local paper presented the story on the front page; the picture they used caught me in a frown and my opponent with a pleasant smile. I won the vote but lost the beauty pageant. I tell the story to encourage all of us to get involved. These were wonderful community leaders, who once they were provided with the opposing evidence in a logical and reasonable manner, were intelligent enough to make a wise decision. I have a dream that someday very soon there will be enough honest statesmen and women in both parties that really understand business, economics, and free-enterprise/capitalism, and have the kinds of values to turn this nation in the right direction.

Years ago, I experienced a sports injury that wasn't healing. A couple of sports doctors tried their various prescriptions, but nothing worked. My wife's gynecologist suggested I try someone who was a chiropractor and naturopath. He gave me a thorough exam suggesting I alter my eating habits. When I followed his more difficult but natural regiment, the injury was healed. I was quite shocked as I began to educate myself and learn the affects of various types of food and how wisdom in this area made so much difference in my health. It began a lifelong educational journey of being responsible for my own health. By reading and learning about how the body worked, I started to make lifestyle changes that have served me well. Instead of waiting for a crisis and then having to trust whatever crisis care my general practitioner had to implement, I was being responsible enough to learn the truth.

Later, in an unrelated incident, a man wanted to reward me by giving me some stock in various companies. I placed the stocks in a brokerage firm and watched the stocks lose a huge amount of their value. Through a series of taking the professional's advice, I lost even more. One day it dawned on me that perhaps my personal savings and investment portfolio required me getting educated in this area like I had done in the health area. After a certain amount of trial and error, my understanding of various investment strategies has made all the difference.

UNFORTUNATELY MOST PEOPLE ARE WOEFULLY UNINFORMED ABOUT THE ECONOMICS OF HOW OUR GOVERNMENT WORKS.

Meanwhile, when conversing with others, I've discovered that most people, even those who are quite responsible in their careers and other areas of their lives, are woefully uninformed about the economics of how our government works. Solomon said, "The rich ruleth over the poor, and the borrower is servant to the lender."[4] For example, three years ago I purchased a car with a zero-percent loan from the car company. I needed a new car; they needed the business and were willing to let me drive "their" car as long as I paid them 367 dollars a month. As an intelligent individual, I figured I would rather invest the full price of the car in other moneymaking ventures and just pay for the car a little bit at a time over three years. Who was I a servant to? I was a servant to the car company because they owned the title until I completely paid off our agreed-upon price. What if I chose to take on additional debt until I reached a point of not being able to make my payment? Of course, they would have repossessed "their" car.

In layman's terms, without getting bogged down with excessive detail, I'll attempt to give a simple explanation for how the U.S. government functions economically. When the U.S. Congress, Senate, and Executive Branch do not balance the budget of the government, where does the money come from? If entitlements such as Medicare, Medicaid, Social Security, and various welfare programs are continually raised and payments are made, where does the money come from? After WWII, in 1944, at Bretton

Woods, New Hampshire, the forty-four allied nations met and decided to establish the U.S. dollar as the world's reserve currency. As a nation, we have an alternative to print more money when we face difficulty and more readily get away with it due to the fact that the dollar is currently the world's reserve currency. However, it lowers the value of the dollar, and we as a nation have to secure investors to buy U.S. treasury bills. Other countries, international mutual funds and investors, and mutual funds and investors within the United States, will invest in U.S. Treasuries if their interest return is significant enough when measured against the risk of us not paying the interest on what we've borrowed. Additionally, any wise investor wants to make sure that the dollar holds its value and that the United States doesn't take on too much debt in proportion to its GDP. The Gross Domestic Product is the monetary value of all the goods and services produced annually within our country's borders, including all of the private and public consumption, government outlays, investments and exports, minus the imports. In other words, do we have a viable strategy for paying off our debts? Have you followed everything so far?

Alarmists really bug me. The last thing I want to do is to act like an alarmist. However, when I put my head on my pillow at night, I want to know I've communicated the truth. The following information is, indeed, alarming and very sobering. It's rather difficult to believe that we have allowed the lion's share of our elected officials to unwisely represent us in the manner they have done. We need to stop whining about the House, the Senate, and the presidency, and we need to take personal responsibility to get educated and hold them accountable. It's our job as American citizens! The government is an extension of us, not our sugar daddy. Coaches that have losing records get fired. The owners and fans are not interested in their rhetoric, good looks, or how they spin all the team's losses. Professional athletes that don't measure up to the requirements of the organization at that time are released, even if they're popular. CEOs that don't increase revenue and make a profit are fired, even if they're in the middle of a contract. Employees that don't effectively fulfill their role in a company are fired, even if they have a family to feed. Essentially, if we pay taxes, we are the shareholders of the U.S. government.

If the borrower is servant to the lender, whom are we serving as a government? Tying it to my personal example, so to speak, who has the authority to repossess the United States' car? Whether we want to or not, we as a government must answer to a whole array of investors. What do I mean? Do we in the USA really want to be a servant to China, Japan, Great Britain, OPEC, Brazil, Taiwan, Caribbean Banking Centers, and Hong Kong? Combined, it's a total of about 5 trillion of our debt owed to foreigners. We are also indebted to just under another trillion to private mutual funds and banks who have to answer to their individual investors. We are also bound by just under another trillion to individual U.S. household investors. We are also a servant to another half trillion to the pension funds of privately held companies. The rest of our debt is related to social security "trust" fund, state and local governments, government related pensions, and finally the largest amount is related to the Federal Reserve and their printing of additional money. Why did Admiral Mullen, the former Joint Chiefs chairman, after a 43-year military career say that our national debt is "the single biggest threat to our national security," and if we don't get control of our debt, there will be a continued loss of confidence in America?[5] What if a very large mutual fund consisting of a large number of foreign investors really analyzes the evidence of our out-of-control spending and decides to conduct an emergency meeting to discuss the matter? Here's what they would discuss:

In our imaginary board meeting, the Chairman of the mutual fund, Fredrick Von Investsmart, begins the meeting by saying, "I found a U.S. Senator serving out his last term because he decided in advance to only serve two terms in the Senate. I figure he is going to call it like it is. He's got nothing to gain or lose. His name is Tom Coburn, M.D. He wrote a book called *The Debt Bomb,* and here is some of what he has observed.

The national debt in the United States may have already passed the tipping point. "In their ground-breaking book about debt and deficits *This Time Is*

Different: Eight Centuries of Financial Folly, economists Carmen Reinhard and Kenneth Rogoff show
that nations whose debt equals 90 percent of their
economy see at best much slower growth and at worst
a total economic collapse."[6] Senator Coburn points
out that at 15 trillion dollars, the U.S. debt is now past
that point (it just passed 16 trillion). Dr. Coburn and
two other senators convinced forty other senators to
attend an early morning presentation from these two
renowned economists. Dr. Coburn writes:

America is already bankrupt. We may not
believe it. We may not yet feel its full effects.
But we are effectively bankrupt. Our debt now
exceeds the size of our entire economy. Our
payments on our obligations, our unfunded
liabilities—exceed our income as far as the
eye can see. No amount of obtainable growth
or tax revenue will be enough. There simply
is no possible way we can finance our long-
term liabilities without fundamentally re-
imagining what government can do in the
twenty-first century."[7]

As Reinhart and Rogoff argue, our economy slows
by 1 point of Gross Domestic Product (GDP) when we
hit a debt-to-GDP ratio of 90 percent, which we hit in
2010.[8] "Using official government estimates, our total
unfunded liabilities are $61.6 trillion."[9] "Medicare and
Social Security alone make up 75 percent of those

liabilities. However, using real-world accounting practices employed by businesses and corporations, called generally accepted accounting principles, or GAAP, Michael Tanner with the CATO Institute estimates our unfunded liabilities may be closer to $119.5 trillion."[10]

Chairman of the Federal Reserve, Ben Bernanke is honest about the math: "By definition, the unsustainable trajectories of deficits and debt that the (Congressional Budget Office) outlines cannot actually happen, because creditors would never be willing to lend to a government whose debt, relative to national income, is rising without limit."[11] The Federal Reserve won't be able to keep interest rates low forever. "If interest rates return to their historic average of about 6 percent, interest payments on the national debt will be the largest line item in the budget by 2020. Interest payments alone on our debt will rise by at least $150 billion per year per point of increase in rates."[12] Dr. Coburn warns, "Top economists have warned me that the world will hit a debt wall and liquidity crisis around 2013, when the world's available liquid assets ($9 trillion) won't be able to meet sovereign debt requirements (about $13 trillion)."[13]

The board meeting continues as some of the board stare off into space while a couple others just shake their head in disgust. One of the members expresses that he saw it coming when the president didn't even accept the bipartisan advice of his own committee of advisors on December 1, 2010. "That was two years ago and the government has continued to spend at such a pace that they borrow $3.5 more billion every single day. The democratic-controlled Senate has voted down three republican budgets intended to reign in spending without offering any alternative whatsoever. The President's budget that he sent to the Senate in 2011 was so unrealistic that it was voted down 97-0. I don't see any alternative but to sell our holdings before the dollar loses any more value and we run the risk of massive losses." Another member asks what the alternative investment is. Most agree that it would be a combination of increasing their holdings in commodities and other currencies. They all can see the wisdom of letting the smoke clear and to take a watch-and-see stance until the United States gets their house in order. Everyone agrees that they will have their chance to re-invest in the United States at much better prices in the future.

What are the chances of something like that happening? What do you think will happen when one of the countries or large mutual funds takes such a step? Have you ever heard of a run on a bank or a sell off in a particular stock such as, Enron™? Once one large holder of U.S. debt makes such a decision, it would obviously trigger a ripple effect. If ever our country needed prayer, it's now. There are so many things that need to happen relatively quickly—it's mind-boggling! A congressional research service concluded:

Many observers are concerned that the large fraction of national debt held by foreigners has the potential to be harmful to the U.S. economy. Specifically, they fear that if foreigners suddenly decided to stop holding U.S. Treasury securities or decided to diversify their holdings, the dollar could plummet in value and interest rates would rise. Others are concerned that the accumulation of U.S. assets by foreign governments, such as China, will give those governments leverage that may be applied to the detriment of U.S. interests. Some economists also argue that foreign borrowing at current levels is unsustainable and could cause problems for the U.S. economy down the road.[14]

Senator Jim DeMint, in his book *Now or Never* observes that:

We are now irresponsibly borrowing 43 cents for every dollar we spend, with no way to pay it back. To make matters worse, America's exploding debt is compounded by the slow growth in tax revenues form a lethargic economy. America's economy is burdened with federal policies that include the highest corporate tax rate in the world, unbridled litigation, and costly regulations. . . . The Small Business Administration's Office of Advocacy stated in September 2010: "The annual cost of federal regulations in the United States increased to more than $1.75 trillion in 2008. Had every U.S. household paid an equal share of the federal regulatory burden, each would have owed $15,586 in 2008."[15]

How is it possible that our government could actually begin to justify that kind of punishment to the very businesses that have the potential to bring down unemployment? A small business in 2008 "spent $10,585 per employee on regulation, which amounts to 36 percent more per employee than their larger counterparts."[16] Why? For what reason? That's just it; there is rarely an overall, big-picture logic chain with our government. Truly, the right hand doesn't seem to know what the left hand is doing. It's simply too big and too disorganized. As President Reagan said, "Government is not a solution to our problem, government is the problem."[17] One CEO testified at a house hearing that an independent manufacturing study by MAPI "estimates that the most stringent ozone proposal being considered would result in the loss of 7.3 million jobs by 2020 and add $1 trillion in new regulatory costs per year between 2020 and 2030."[18] Shouldn't we be trying to create more manufacturing jobs instead of eliminate them? Kevin Rogers, president of the Arizona Farm Bureau Federation and a fourth-generation farmer testified about "new" regulations at a house hearing, "It is no exaggeration to say that the onslaught of federal regulations now confronting farmers and ranchers across America is truly overwhelming . . . . The EPA estimates over 37,000 agricultural facilities will be covered, at an average cost of more than $23,200 per permit, resulting in costs of over $866 million to producers."[19] If Sherlock Holmes were to investigate, he might conclude that a logical analysis of the case appears to indicate the sabotaging of American business. However, with the regulations, at least the ignorant masses are being protected from the horrifying dangers of little kids setting up lemonade stands. In five different states, taking their cues from the federal government, "children's lemonade stands have been shut down and the parents fined up to $500."[20] After all, these young entrepreneurs must be nipped in the bud; they're liable to grow up, start a business, and employ thousands! It's no wonder Americans are pausing from their busy schedules to join their neighbors for a tea party.

Meanwhile, every king, queen, prime minister, president, dictator, judge, senator, congressional representative, chairman and governing official has to answer to the combined authority of the free-market economy. There is no country or government that is too big to fail. If a government becomes over-confident, irresponsible and unwise, it will lose the investing confidence of the free market. Even those organizations that think they have banded together with some sort of manipulative and controlling influence, will eventually find they were merely stooges for yet another group of even higher powerbrokers. It would be comical if it weren't so detrimental for the bigger picture of humanity at large. Freedom-loving, wise men and women who are well-prepared to step up and restore intelligent rule of law leadership, are waiting in the wings for the unwise to exhaust their many and sundry discretionary ideas.

Like it or not, America is under the watchful eye of a whole host of international and national investors, which is exactly why the rule of law must be followed. To depart from the economic and monetary wisdom of the rule of law is a recipe of suicidal proportions. No amount of babble, chatter, yapping, jabber, drivel, and blabber is going to enable this nation to pass the test of its investors. Only responsible rule-of-law results and sacrifice will win.

Breaking down the specific amounts for educational purposes may drive home the point. Each individual lender has trusted the United States to place a certain amount of money at stake and at risk. To some degree, we must impress the following investors with our fiscal responsibility. Listed from the largest to the smallest lender, the first number is the total amount our nation has borrowed from the investor listed and the number in parentheses is the total percent of the United State's overall debt to that lender. The Social Security Trust Fund 2.67 trillion (19%) at stake (unbelievable that we have borrowed money from Social Security), the Federal Reserve with 1.63 trillion

(11.3%) at stake, China with 1.16 trillion (8%) at stake, United States households 959.4 billion (6.6%) at stake, Japan with 912.4 billion (6.4%) at stake, state and local governments 506.1 billion (3.5%) at stake, private pension funds 504.7 billion (3.5%) at stake, United Kingdom 346.5 billion (2.4%) at stake, money market mutual funds 337.7 billion (2.4%) at stake, state, local, and federal retirement funds 320.9 billion (2.2%) at stake, commercial banks 301.8 billion (2.1%) at stake, mutual funds 300.5 billion (2%) at stake, OPEC 229.8 billion (1.6%) at stake, Brazil 211.4 billion (1.5%) at stake, Taiwan 153.4 billion (1.1%) at stake, Caribbean banking centers 148.3 billion (1%) at stake, Hong Kong 121.9 billion (.9%) at stake.[21] America owes foreigners about a third of our debt, around $5 trillion. Notwithstanding, America owes America about $10 trillion.

"I believe that banking institutions are more dangerous to our liberties than standing armies. Already they have raised up a monied aristocracy that has set the government at defiance. The issuing power (of money) should be taken away from the banks and restored to the people to whom it properly belongs."[I]
—THOMAS JEFFERSON

"The [Federal Reserve Act] as it stands seems to me to open the way to a vast inflation of the currency. . . . I do not like to think that any law can be passed that will make it possible to submerge the gold standard in a flood of irredeemable paper currency."[II]
—HENRY CABOT LODGE, SR.

"The financial system has been turned over to the Federal Reserve Board. That Board administers the finance system by authority of a purely profiteering group. The system is Private, conducted for the sole purpose of obtaining the greatest possible profits from the use of other people's money."[III]
—CHARLES A. LINDBERGH, SR.

5

Bankers, Gold, and Jekyll Island

There is a great temptation to complicate life and feel the need to come up with the latest, newest discretionary analysis. I'm all for imploring the sound rules of logic to solve problems, and modernity has affected and compromised good sound reasoning that's based on the rule of law. Rather, I'm referring to the idea of continually placing Band-Aids™ on problems because of the latest research that our information age has produced. We arrogantly assume that new information is the secret rather than age-old execution of proven wisdom from solid dependable documents.

I'm referring to written documentation from a solid source. It's the true north, the origin, genesis, fountainhead, starting point, or ground zero that you can return to over and over to provide leadership when the storms of life are raging. The details can be managed along the way, but the vision and the direction is established by your source document. Solomon specifically addresses what we're discussing, "The thing that hath been, it is that which shall be; and that which is done is that which shall be done: and there is no new thing under the sun."[1]

Certainly new technology dramatically impacts our lives. However, the inventions that matter the most simply speed up the process of doing something or make the task more convenient or pleasurable. Calculators have saved me time and trees, but the main problem of needing to crunch numbers hasn't changed. I take great delight in garage door openers, but the end-result goal hasn't changed: get the door open! Smartphones are new technology, but the value of communication is age-old.

Two plus two is four whether it's a rainy day or the sun is shining. Being certain of the arithmetic tables opens the door to deeper mathematical truths. Knowing the precise meaning of a word enables you to use the word in the right way. Dictionaries come in quite handy for articulating a message in a way that everyone can clearly follow. Arithmetic tables and dictionaries are source documents that can be depended on. Imagine if I were to wake up some day and decide to use my personal discretion concerning two plus two. On some weeks, I decide the answer is five; while on other weeks, I determine the answer to be back to four. Sounds rather silly, doesn't it? There has been a breakdown in society holding the highest possible value to the source documents that provide the foundation for the rule and law in various areas. Rules and laws that originate from a solid source document will eventually produce effective results over and over if persisted with.

The United States has the source documents of the Declaration of Independence and the Constitution that were designed to serve as a boundary for legislators to function within its guidelines. These source documents have already been agreed on in advance, prior to any individual problem that requires a solution. The documents lay out a system of rules and principles that are required to be followed in the process of governing. In theory, although violated in day-to-day governing, government authorities are supposed to abide by these documents.

I came across an unnerving editorial in *Investor's Business Daily* that illustrates the point of disregarding a source document:

Two top Democrats in Congress say the legislature doesn't really need to pass a budget. Excuse us, but passing a budget isn't optional; it's required by law . . . . Actually, "the fact is," Congress is required under the Congressional Budget and Impoundment Control Act of 1974 to pass a spending plan and then have it scored by the Congressional Budget Office and signed by the president. That none of this happens suggests a level of disrespect for the law and the people found only among criminals . . . . Stunning indeed. It's now been 1,020 days, or 2.8 years, since Congress last passed a budget. Rather than an official document, Congress has passed a series of continuing resolutions and spending bills, periodically raising the debt ceiling so it can spend even more.[2]

THE IDEA OF INDIVIDUALS ELECTED TO WRITE AND OVERSEE OUR LAWS SHOWING SUCH CONTEMPT FOR THE DOCUMENT THEY SWORE TO UPHOLD IS INDEED UNNERVING!

The idea of individuals elected to write and oversee our laws showing such contempt for the document they swore to uphold is indeed unnerving!

The various branches within our government have moved to a more discretionary approach to solving problems. Even their discretion doesn't abide by sound rules of logic. The dictionary defines discretionary as "available for use at the discretion of the user: rules are inevitably less flexible than a discretionary policy."[3] In other words, a group of supposedly wise men and women use their insight to solve a particular problem that may or may not be based on a set of rules and principles that have already been established beforehand. They are not restricting themselves by any set framework of rules, laws or principles that they must abide by.

A perfect example of a group of people getting educated about the rule of law as it pertains to monetary policy can be seen in the popularity of Ron Paul. I've watched with amazement as a generation of young people have paid attention to a 76-year-old man, Ron Paul, that has the unmitigated gall to suggest that the

USA stop the insanity of printing money and dishing out that printed money on every whim politicians decide to spend it on. Many young people are having the nerve to agree with his bold vision to actually move the country back toward some semblance of the gold standard. Prior to President Nixon taking us off the gold standard in 1971, the United States for nearly 200 years had maintained at least 25 percent of gold on hand to satisfy Federal Reserve notes. This, of course, is an excellent example of the rule of law versus discretionary policy. The rule is to limit the amount of dollars printed to what can be backed up with a certain amount of gold. A dollar today can buy only one-sixth of what it could buy in 1971. Inflation, which had averaged less than 2 percent when America began edging away from the gold standard in 1967, has averaged 4.5 percent between 1967 and 2009.[4]

I spent a week consulting and teaching a leadership course to the department heads of the very Georgia resort on Jekyll Island that was the location of the secret meeting in 1913 to conceive and plan the birth of the Federal Reserve. My hosts explained the history and saga of the secret meeting as long as I would not divulge the information to the ignorant masses. I must confess that the part of divulging the information is just a joke, but it was rather eerie to sit and read a book on the origin of the Federal Reserve Act in the very room that supposedly the seven men, who represented an estimated one-fourth of the total wealth of the entire world, actually met.

On the same note, another example of the rule of law relates to the age-old pattern of markets correcting themselves versus the insertion of government officials trying to fix basic fluctuations that regularly occur. For example, Keynesianism is applying discretionary government intervention of monetary policy theory. John Maynard Keynes theorized, "There is no natural tendency for capitalist market economies . . . to correct economic shocks and maintain an equilibrium at full employment. Before Keynes, it was well known that there was a regular pattern of boom and slump, but it was assumed that economies quickly righted themselves without government intervention. Keynes denied this."[5] In short, Keynes had a new discretionary idea "under the sun" that assumed the historical track record of the marketplace regulating itself was not adequate. Obviously, I'm not implying that governments cannot, on very rare occasions, apply a minimal and temporary measure when a major crisis occurs.

THE ONLY WAY TO CHANGE OUR NATION IS WITH AN EDUCATED AND INTELLIGENT POPULACE THAT BASES THEIR LIVES ON SOUND LAWS AND PRINCIPLES.

However, the stakes are too high for all of us to blindly follow government officials, without educating ourselves concerning these types of departures from the rule of law in favor of the modernity of discretionary ideas. Remember, America is a republic!

The key always comes down to execution of the fundamentals

rather than assuming that something new must be found. The only way to change our nation is with an educated and intelligent populace that bases their lives on solid rules, laws and principles. I've continually guided the clients I've worked with in the direction of solid rules and principles that have endured the test of time. When they face the various tests and difficulties that life brings, they automatically return to their true-north that gets them back on track.

One example is Les. He has found that returning to the principles and character objectives he has established has continually served him well. He returns to his pre-determined goals and says them over and over. He directs his life by painting an accurate and specific image, and then he reaffirms it whenever setbacks occur. It's not unusual for people to set out on a course and then give up when the various trials pop up. I've always made it clear to clients to persist with the fundamental principles and eventually they'll be pleased with the results. Les is another one of those leaders that has schooled himself on putting people first. Time and time again he is there above and beyond the call of duty to help one of his employees. In his insurance company, you can always depend on the integrity and honesty of their quotes and their way of conducting business. His charitable giving is another area that is key to his heart. He has taken the principles and can be often found teaching what he has learned to others.

"But if in the pursuit of the means we should unfortunately stumble again on unfunded paper money or any similar species of fraud, we shall assuredly give a fatal stab to our national credit in its infancy. Paper money will invariably operate in the body of politics as spirit liquors on the human body. They prey on the vitals and ultimately destroy them. Paper money has had the effect in your state that it will ever have, to ruin commerce, oppress the honest, and open the door to every species of fraud and injustice."[I]
—GEORGE WASHINGTON

"Most Americans have no real understanding of the operation of the international money lenders. The accounts of the Federal Reserve System have never been audited. It operates outside the control of Congress and manipulates the credit of the United States."[II]
—SEN. BARRY GOLDWATER

"It is well that the people of the nation do not understand our banking and monetary system, for if they did, I believe there would be a revolution before tomorrow morning."[III]
—HENRY FORD

"Whoever controls the volume of money in any country is absolute master of all industry and commerce."[IV]
—JAMES A. GARFIELD

6

Money Madness = $16 Trillion and Climbing

How does the rule of law affect the economic policies of our nation? Nobel Prize winner Milton Friedman, in his 1962 classic *Capitalism and Freedom,* argued for economic policies based on "a government of law instead of men" because of the first amendment to the Constitution and the complete Bill of Rights.[1] Over sixty years earlier, Friedrich Hayek wrote:

Nothing distinguishes more clearly conditions in a free country from those in a country under arbitrary government than the observation in the former of the great principles known as the Rule of Law. Stripped of all technicalities, this means that government in all its actions is bound by rules fixed and announced beforehand—rules which make it possible to foresee with fair certainty how the authority will use its coercive powers in given circumstances and to plan one's individual affairs on the basis of this knowledge.[2]

Stanford professor John Taylor identifies three more Nobel Prize winning economists in his book, *First Principles,* that highlight the wisdom of the Rule of Law. Finn Kydland and Edward Prescott showed that discretionary policies produce poor results by denying people the benefits of policy commitments. Robert Lucas identified that clear policy rules are needed to determine how a particular economic policy would work. Businesses are dependent on knowing both the policy today and in the future before they can plan and make wise decisions. Discretionary policies break down because people don't know what they can depend on in the future.[3]

Our government should have paid attention to the work of these individuals instead of managing from crisis to crisis with various discretionary ideas. Most elected officials have thought more highly of their discretionary notions than they should have. They have made it extremely difficult for businesses to be secure with their multi-year goals because they have no idea what the latest government brainchild will end up being. Set, rule-of-law polices that are not up for the latest discretionary whims of a current crop of elected politicians would provide a level and consistent playing field that politicians would have to manage the government within set boundaries.

Free markets are willing to take risks, whether it's hiring people or rolling out a new product when uncertainty is lifted and replaced with some degree of certainty, barring a major disaster within the country. Many other distinguished individuals could be identified as touting the merits of the rule of law, policy predictability or proven principles as a foundation for sound decision-making. Sometimes it means facing temporary pain for long-term, positive results. Your delayed gratification today sets the stage for you to experience future victory. It's the idea of no pain, no gain.

Let's look at a specific example within our government. It's quite embarrassing to go to usdebtclock.org and watch the debt continuously grow at a mind-boggling pace. Anyone who has ever faced the day-to-day responsibility of living on a budget, scratches his or her head at such a site. In October of 2012, the national debt was $16.215 trillion. It takes 28 seconds for it to go up another million! The personal debt per citizen is $50,913, and the debt per taxpayer is $140,017. In reality, an individual can work two jobs and live very sacrificially to become debt free, only to find that they can't actually be debt free unless the collective team of our government is debt free. Either we win as a nation, or we lose as a nation, pure and simple.

John Taylor, professor at Stanford writes that in 2011, federal spending was $3.6 trillion and revenues were $2.3 trillion, which was about the same in 2010. The federal government is actually borrowing more than one-third of what it spends. "At a projected 75 percent in 2012, the debt has already surpassed the worrisome 60 percent of GDP threshold . . . . The growing debt increases the risks of a financial crisis of the kind seen in Europe in 2011 and in many emerging-market countries in the 1990s."[4] The idea of borrowing over 63 percent of our revenues in 2011 and the projected 75 percent in 2012 is madness. The madness is even greater when you understand that the total national debt is over 100 percent of GDP. You can see a basic violation of the rule and law of spending more money than you take in. Decisions based on discretionary ideas instead of rule-of-law monetary policy by our elected politicians have demonstrated much irresponsibility. In fact, it has displayed massive mathematical insanity!

It's not only our elected politicians that are following discretionary notions but the Federal Reserve has also diverted to discretionary ideas, instead of the dependability of the rule of law. The strong and stable economy of the 1980s and 1990s was largely related to monetary policy conducted in a predictable and rule-like manner. Prior to that, in the 1970s, there were a series of discretionary increases and decreases in money growth and interest rates that led to high inflation, high unemployment and low economic growth. The same thing happened when the Federal Reserve kept interest rates too low for too long in 2003-2005, and it triggered excesses in housing and other markets, which brought on the boom followed by the bust. The fed's continuing departure from a rules-based monetary policy has increased the economic instability. Meanwhile, countries like Mexico, Brazil and Poland have been moving away from their discretionary policies of the 1980s and 1990s toward more rule-like policies and are experiencing improved results, especially when compared to the U.S. and Europe.[5]

I'm not necessarily intending to be critical of the majority of Federal Reserve officials. They have a hard job, they're quite smart, and they're certainly trying to help the economy with their discretionary ideas. However, there are descending views among the various fed officials, along with those outside the government such as John Taylor, who are convinced that it's far greater wisdom to move us more toward rule-of-law, monetary policies. It has been said over and over that the crisis of 2007-2008 was such that extreme discretionary measures were required for such a monumental crisis. I know these are good men applying their brainpower and discretion to do the best they can with massive economic problems. I'm merely identifying how hard it is to use discretion instead of the rule of law as they walk the tightrope of their dual mandate of trying to keep both maximum employment and stable prices as their goals.

The dual mandate happened in 1977 when President Carter amended the Federal Reserve Act of 1913 and established the fed's dual mandate. Up until then, they had the single focus of keeping inflation under control. We have given far too much authority to an unelected body of Fed officials that

WE HAVE GIVEN FAR TOO MUCH AUTHORITY TO AN UNELECTED BODY OF FED OFFICIALS.

are using their discretion instead of established rules of monetary policy. Like so many of the other problems in our government, we're not willing to face the temporary pain to allow the free market to regulate itself. The rule of law would declare that lesser pain today is better than catastrophic pain later. Guess what we're setting up ourselves for? Since the Congress has the responsibility to "coin Money, regulate the Value thereof" under Article I, Section 8, of the Constitution, it seems wise for them to restore and lock in consistent rule-based policies that have worked over time and avoid discretionary policies that have no or a minimal historical track record. While Congress is at it, they now have additional history to evaluate the wisdom of returning the Federal Reserve to the sole mandate of just keeping inflation under control. This would make it less tempting for the damaging policy swings toward discretion.[6]

Stanford professor John Taylor identifies the hard choices that Paul Volcker made from 1979-1982 in the midst of much economic pain that helped set the stage for two decades of steady economic growth. Although he had the dual mandate, he chose to focus on getting inflation under control even though unemployment was high. During the pain of 14.6 percent inflation in March of 1980, Volcker was resolute to their agreed-upon rules; and President Reagan was just as resolute in his support of him. Inflation was down to 8.9 percent in December of 1981 and 3.8 percent by the end of 1982. It took courage for Volcker and Reagan to stick to their principles in the midst of difficulty for the sake of future success.[7]

Once again, I'm no economist, but I can read a history book. I can read the various economic theories of great minds and then utilize the rules of logic and the results of history to arrive at a conclusion. What monetary policies have proven historical results? Use those principles and stick to them even if it means facing pain today to avoid greater pain in the future. Thomas Edison said:

"Genius? Nothing! Sticking to it is the genius! Any other bright-minded fellow can accomplish just as much if he will stick like hell and remember: nothing that's any good works by itself. You've got to make the damn thing work!"[8] Instead of being intellectually overconfident and leaning too much on more and more discretionary ideas, it seems the better part of wisdom to settle on sound rule-of-law principles and stick with them. Milton Friedman said, "The best is often the enemy of the good . . . . The attempts to do more than we can will itself be a disturbance that may increase rather than reduce instability."[9]

The stakes are too high for all of us to blindly follow the failed policies of certain politicians and government officials. After all, America is a republic. That means that problems in my government are as much my fault as those who are representing me and making decisions on my behalf. If I point the finger at them, I have three more pointing back at myself. The problems in our nation start and end with you and me as individuals. The only way to change our nation is with an educated and intelligent populace that bases our lives on solid rules, laws and principles.

Ronald Reagan cautioned us, "Freedom is never more than one generation away from extinction. We didn't pass it to our children in the bloodstream. It must be fought for, protected, and handed on for them to do the same, or one day we will spend our sunset years telling our children and our children's children what it was once like in the United States where men were free."[10] Mark Levin, in his book *Ameritopia: The Unmaking of America*, explains the heart of the problem in our nation,

> Utopianism is the ideological and doctrinal foundation for statism . . . . Indeed, the modern arguments about the necessities and virtues of government control over the individual are but malign echoes of utopian prescriptions through the ages, which attempted to define subjugation as the most transcendent state of man. Utopianism has long promoted the idea of a paradisiacal existence and advanced concepts of pseudo "ideal" societies in which a heroic despot, a benevolent sovereign, or an enlightened oligarchy claims the ability and authority to provide for all the needs and fulfill all the wants of the individual—in exchange for his abject servitude.[11]

In other words, the discretionary ideas of a few are supposedly wiser than the age-old principles of truth, liberty and the rule of law. Turning our country around is not for the fainthearted or the passive that seem content to refer to the problems in our government as "they and them." How about "we and us"? Remember, "we the people"?

It's time to borrow a few lines from the Notre Dame fight song. Father, forgive me for my alteration of some of the words. "Wake up the echoes. Send a volley cheer on high . . . . Shake down the thunder from the sky. What though the odds be great or small . . . (faithful, God honoring, freedom-loving men and women) . . . will win over all, While her loyal sons (and daughters) . . . are marching Onward to victory."[12] Indeed we must wake up the great echoes of this nation!

According to the New Oxford American Dictionary, a zombie is "a person who is or appears lifeless, apathetic, or completely unresponsive to their surroundings."[13] Let's believe that millions of Americans will awaken from any zombie-like states and become razor sharp in understanding the important issues of free-enterprise/capitalism and the rule of law and that they become quick to respond to any irresponsible decisions within their government.

Thomas Jefferson said, "The natural progress of things is for liberty to yield, and government to gain ground."[14] Oh by the way, Jefferson also said, "I consider the fortunes of our republic as depending, in an eminent degree, on the extinguishment of public debt."[15]

"I have never seen more Senators express discontent with their jobs . . . I think the major cause is that, deep down in our hearts, we have been accomplices in doing something terrible and unforgivable to our wonderful country. Deep down in our heart, we know that we have given our children a legacy of bankruptcy. We have defrauded our country to get ourselves elected."[I]
—JOHN DANFORTH (R-MO)

"Practically all government attempts to redistribute wealth and income tend to smother productive incentives and lead toward general impoverishment. It is the proper sphere of government to create and enforce a framework of law that prohibits force and fraud. But it must refrain from specific economic interventions. Government's main economic function is to encourage and preserve a free market."[II]
—HENRY HAZLITT

7

Coming out of the Asylum— Simpson and Bowles

The president established a non-partisan commission that first met in April 2010, intended to establish policies to improve the fiscal situation in the medium term and to achieve fiscal sustainability over the long run. Democrat Erskine Bowles, the former chief of staff for President Clinton, and former senator Alan Simpson, republican from Wyoming, chaired the meeting. After convening for months, the commission settled on a proposal on December 1, 2010, that would reduce the deficit by $4 trillion over ten years. The plan would cut spending by "$3 trillion and generate $1 trillion in revenue through reducing tax rates and eliminating spending in the tax code."[1] There were eighteen members on the commission, eleven supported it, which was three votes short of the fourteen required to report their findings, but they nonetheless reported their findings. Senator Coburn, one of the commission members that although supporting the plan, said, "This plan is a plan . . . I have heartache with tons of it, but I know we have to go forward. This is just the down payment."[2] He made the point that it did not reform Medicare, which was by far the biggest driver of the deficits. The democrats on the commission were unwilling to reopen the contentious debate on health care. Nevertheless, all three senate republicans on the commission, Coburn, Mike Crapo and Judd Gregg supported it. Senator Coburn writes how unfortunate it was that the president "refused to embrace the recommendations and offered almost no feedback . . . . As the year unfolded, Simpson-Bowles would remain the high-water mark of bipartisan deficit reduction efforts."[3]

I can understand why Coburn had "heartache with tons of it" because it needs to be far bolder when we're over $16 trillion in debt. To take ten years to only lower the debt $4 trillion dollars is quite feeble in spending cuts. I understand the need to negotiate, but as I'll get to shortly, it's hard to compromise with poor math. If Medicare were off the table to begin with, then we're not really intelligently facing the mathematical truth as I'll demonstrate in a moment. Having said that, at least it is stopping the increases and starting some semblance of reducing the debt, be it ever so infinitesimal. We've got to at least start and do something.

Dr. Coburn went on to serve on the gang of six to try to put the Simpson-Bowles report into legislative language. In 2011, House Budget Committee Chairman Paul Ryan offered a detailed plan of his own taking the best of Simpson-Bowles along with reforming Medicare, but "third-party groups funded by liberal donors started running ads featuring a Paul Ryan lookalike

ANYBODY THAT SAYS WE (CONGRESS) DON'T LOOK LIKE FOOLS UP HERE HASN'T READ THE REPORT.

pushing a senior in a wheelchair off a cliff. The Democratic establishment's decision to demagogue Medicare sent a clear signal that the party was not remotely serious about entitlement reform."[4] Things were moving so slowly, Dr. Coburn released his own list of recommendations entitled "Back in Black," in which he outlined $9 trillion in savings from across the entire federal budget. It's not as hard as one might think when you consider the Government Accountability Office (GAO) 2011 report showing that we "are spending trillions of dollars every year, and nobody knows what we are doing. The executive branch doesn't know. Congress doesn't know. Nobody knows."[5] Senator Coburn commented about the report to a group of reporters saying that the findings due out the next day would make "all of us look like jackasses . . . . Anybody that says we don't look like fools up here hasn't read the report."[6] The report can be read at http://gao.gov/new.items/d11318sp.pdf entitled "Opportunities to Reduce Potential Duplication in Government Programs, Save Tax Dollars, and Enhance Revenue." It contains things such as: nine federal agencies spend approximately $18 billion annually to administer forty-seven job-training programs (it was unclear if any worked); twenty separate agencies run fifty-six different financial literacy programs (why Congress

> THERE HAS BEEN MUCH TALK IN CONGRESS ABOUT BUSINESSES THAT ARE TO BIG TO FAIL AND NEED TO BE DIVIDED UP. THAT'S A GREAT IDEA FOR THE FEDERAL GOVERNMENT.

believes it is qualified to teach financial literacy is beyond me); ten agencies run eighty-two teacher-training programs, while fifteen agencies monitor food safety. One agency manages cheese pizza (FDA), but if you buy a pepperoni pizza, that's another agency (USDA), further reinforcement that the right hand doesn't know what the left hand is doing. There is much talk in the House, Senate and Executive Branch about businesses that are too big to fail and need to be divided up. That's a great idea for the federal government.

Mathematics becomes very important in the matter of a budget and financially wise management. Let's look at the obvious mathematical facts of exactly what we're dealing with as it pertains to Medicare's impact on the deficit. Are you aware that when President Franklin Roosevelt signed Social Security into law, the average life expectancy was 64 and the earliest retirement age was 65? Today, the average life expectancy for Americans is seventy-eight; they retire three years earlier and spend twenty years in retirement. In 1950, there were sixteen workers for every recipient of social security. Guess what it is today? The ratio of workers to recipients is 3 to 1.[7] The average couple has put about $120,000 toward Medicare during their working life, but they take out $350,000.[8] Any elected official that refuses to talk about and tackle the obvious math of entitlements is either delusional or outright dishonest. We need elected officials that will courageously tell the truth, so help them God.

In the movie *The Right Stuff,* John Glenn's (played by Ed Harris) heat shield on his spacecraft becomes dysfunctional, which will affect re-entering the earth's atmosphere. The scientists debate when and how to communicate the bad news, and Alan Shepherd (played by Scott Glenn) passionately says that John Glenn is a pilot, and he deserves to know the condition of his craft. In the same way, we the people deserve to know the magnitude of the problem of entitlements. We need to hear from both parties the words spoken of our elected representatives, directly, honestly, and without cowardice. Particularly, our senior citizens deserve the truth. They are the prized possession of our nation, and many have survived the Depression, WWII, and plenty of other sacrifices along the way. These are men and women made of special stuff by the trials and challenges of life they have had to face. In fact, it wouldn't surprise me to see a grassroots movement among them to send a message to Washington to get our house in order for the sake of their grandchildren and great grandchildren. Senator Coburn talks about town-hall meetings he's had with senior citizens in which every single one of them have said they will sacrifice and do their part to restore Medicare and Social Security.

Senator Joe Lieberman joined Senator Tom Coburn with a proposal to deal with Medicare. Coburn said

Lieberman's address was one of the most moving and common sense speeches he had heard about the need for congress to make tough choices. Part of his speech was:

> The biggest, but not only, drivers of the debt are entitlements, including Medicare. So if we don't deal with those entitlements, we won't ever balance our budget . . . . Each Medicare beneficiary will, on the average, take almost three times more out in Medicare benefits than they put in in payroll taxes and premiums. That's why we say that the status quo in Medicare is unsustainable. What we mean is that if we do nothing, Medicare will go broke and take our government down with it . . . we can't save Medicare as we know it. We can only save Medicare if we change it . . . . If there ever were a time in American history for elected officials to stop thinking about the next election and start thinking about the next generation, it is now.[9]

Anybody that understands basic arithmetic can figure out that a plan designed for sixteen workers paying in for every recipient cannot be sustained when there are only three workers paying in for each recipient. Plus, each recipient is living fourteen years longer than when the program was set up. Those courageous men and women who sound the alarm set themselves up as targets because nobody "likes" to take unpleasant-tasting medicine. Yet, we've all faced disappointing setbacks, and although we might whine and complain, eventually we all would rather know the truth when a problem had some kind of a hopeful correction rather than waiting until there's a sudden monumental catastrophe. Obviously, this should have been faced along the way every year in each new budget. It would be an interesting book for some enterprising author to go back and find the elected officials that were wise and honest through the years on this subject. I'll bet there were always men and women who were sounding the alarm but voted down by those who were more out for re-election than straightforward mathematical integrity. Once they are identified, we could establish a hall of fame for honest, straightforward politicians, which would in turn give every aspiring future politician something to shoot for.

Amazingly, right when I was working on this section I stumbled across a wonderful interview with Simpson and Bowles on July 12, 2012. Becky Quick interviewed Erskin Bowles, Alan Simpson and Warren Buffet. Buffet and Bowles are democrats, and they positioned the witty republican Simpson in the middle. As far as I'm concerned, on this particular day, I heard three stellar Americans sound the alarm for us to get our debt under control. The interview began with Buffet saying that 80 to 90 percent of the CEOs around the country are for Simpson-Bowles and cannot understand why our government didn't follow through and enact the recommendations. It was delightful to listen to Simpson, a republican, praise his co-chairman Bowles, a democrat, calling him "a giant among pygmies" in his ability to deal with numbers. Buffet chimed in:

They sat down with republicans and democrats, and they were given a charge to come up with a plan that . . . got it down to 3 percent of GDP. And they got it down below that. They got a majority of the republicans to vote for it. They got 11 out of 18. They did exactly what they'd been asked to do. And they came up with a plan. No plan is perfect. You know, everybody can come up with a little different one. But everybody knows that we need something done."

Then Bowles said:

I think if I had to tell you the probability, I'd say the chances are we're goin' over the fiscal cliff. And, I hate to say it, but I think that's probably right. But we've worked hard to try to—to get common sense to overrule politics. And that's a tough thing in Washington, as Al can tell ya. But we've been around—the Senate and the House. We probably have as many as 45 to 47 senators, equal number of republicans and democrats who are in support of our efforts. We've got about 150 House members, again relatively equal. We've put together a CEO fiscal leadership council, which has over 100 Fortune 500 CEOs who are actively working to try to influence Congress to do something that makes just plain common sense. And we've got a social media campaign that we're workin' on where we hope to get—about 10 million signatures of people around the country to tell Congress, "Come on, let's put partisanship aside, and let's pull together, and let's face this enormous fiscal problem that we have comin' up.

Bowles added what he said to a graduating class:

I said they oughta be mad at us, at our generation for shirkin' our responsibilities and kickin' the can down the road. We've gotta face up to this. I mean, this is our generation's problem. And we gotta fix it . . . . And for me, the best analogy is these deficits are like a cancer. And over time, they will destroy the country from within. Here's an easy way to understand it from a math viewpoint. If you take last year, 100 percent of our revenue that came into the country, every nickel, every single dollar that came into the country last year was spent on— what's called mandatory spending and interest on the debt. Mandatory spending is principally the entitlement programs: Medicare, Medicaid, and Social Security. What that means is every single dollar we spent last year on these two wars, national defense, homeland security, education, infrastructure, high-value-added research, every single dollar was borrowed. And half of it was borrowed from foreign countries. That is crazy. Crazy. It's a formula for failure in any organization . . . we're spendin' right now $250 billion a year on interest at these incredibly low rates. That's more, to put it in perspective, than we spend if the Department of Commerce, Education, Energy, Homeland Security, Justice, Interior, and State combined. And if interest rates were at their average level in the 1990s or the first decade of this century we'd be spending over $650 billion.

Becky pointed out, "But the president also didn't act and didn't follow up with what he had set out. Who do you blame for where we are right now?"

Simpson responded with:

Well, we try to stay away from the blame game—people will often say, 'How did we get here?' It's easy how we got here. We were told to bring home the bacon for the last seventy years. Go get the highway, go get me some money, go get—raise this, do this, do that. And you got reelected by bringin' home the bacon—and now the pig is dead . . . . And one of our members,

Dick Durbin . . . voted for this and Tom Coburn. Two fine, splendid men with totally different ideologies and philosophies on politics. And everyone kept sayin', "Where's the tipping point?" And that's the key. Because when the tipping point comes and the guys who give us money want more money for their money, then inflation will kick in and—all these things, and interest. And guess who will be hurt the worst? The little guy that everybody talks about day and night. What fakery. What phoniness.

Bowles pointed out:

You know, we don't spare anything. I mean . . . the problem is so big right now that, you know . . . you have to make significant cuts in defense. You have to make significant cuts in the entitlement programs. You have to make significant cuts in the spending in the tax code if you're gonna produce enough deficit reduction to stabilize the debt.

Simpson joined in about defense:

This is madness. $750, $760 billion is the USA . . . . Russia and China combined spend $540 billion . . . . I'm a veteran. I was proud to serve. There's a thing called Tri-Care. And it's for military retirees . . . . And some of them have had very little active duty, but they've been in the Guard or the Reserve. They have their own health care plan. And the premium is 470 bucks a year. And no co-pay. Takes care of all dependents and costs us $53 billion a year.

Bowles adds, "Here's how crazy defense is. Just think about this. The United States has a treaty with Taiwan that we'll protect Taiwan if they're invaded by the Chinese. There's only one problem with that. We gotta borrow the money from China to do it." Bowles then brought up health care, "The entitlements are a big part of what we have to focus on. And what we've been tryin' to do is figure out how we can slow the rate of growth—in health care—to the rate of growth of . . . the economy."

Buffet added, "You can over-promise. And that's what we've done. And—you have to get your promises in line with your capacity."

Bowles went further:

And today not only are our promises too big, but our outcomes are not so great. You take health care. We spend twice as much as any other country in the world on health care. The way we talk about it is—on a per capita basis or a percent of GDP. And you know, that might be okay if our outcomes were twice as good as anybody else's. But on outcome . . . almost any

outcome measure you look at, we rank some-
where between 25th and 50th in things like
infant mortality and life expectancy and
preventable death.[10]

Unfortunately, those with enough integrity to face
the critical music of trying to cut expenses have faced
the wrath of interest groups who are perfectly satisfied to holler, "Nobody's going to take our piece of the
pie of government money away from us!"

I gathered from the spirit of this interview that
they each felt the cuts should be far greater due to the
magnitude of the crisis. Various interest groups have
tremendously criticized Simpson and Bowles for
touching their sacred area, but they have courageously pressed on, along with Senator Coburn and
Paul Ryan with their various plans. Once the president didn't support the findings of the commission he
set up, very few were willing to put their vote out
there on the line because of the very interest groups
that would work to unseat them. The ego-self is far
too interested in self-interest than to courageously
stand in the face of criticism for what's genuinely
right. It can be hard to find the Mr. Smiths who have
gone to Washington. It's a little easier to spot the egos
that mislead (or outright lie) to divert attention else-
where, cheat, embellish, bicker or do anything to
protect their turfs. America is in great need of a
miracle within people of authority in this area.

There are no problems our government faces that honesty and integrity cannot correct. However, politicians driven by their ego-self instead of the rule of mathematical law are incapable of the kind of wise character that is required for the numerous "tough-medicine" challenges that need to be tackled and articulated. Please, may we be spared of all the worthless babble of blame shifting and capitalizing on the chance to criticize the hard choices that some politicians have the guts to face. It's the oldest deceit in the book to attack common-sense solutions by taking the opposing view just for the sake of discrediting an opponent. For example, producing a TV commercial of pushing granny over the cliff ought to cause "we the people" to rise up in outrage. No credible solution was offered, just attacking the one person who had the guts to be honest about the enormous virus of government spending. It's so elementary and childish.

WE THE PEOPLE ARE READY TO PUT THE PAST POLITICAL FOOLISHNESS TO REST AND EMBARK ON A FISCALLY RESPONSIBLE PATH.

Also, we're not stupid; we can all see that many republicans, right along with the democrats, over the years have run up debt and not tackled these issues. The various tea-party representatives seem to be among those who are the most courageous to actually tell the truth and hold both parties' feet to the fire. I don't mean to be picking sides when I'm pleading for cooperation; it's just that these are the ones who seem to be disturbing a status quo that certainly needs to be disturbed. We the people beg our representatives to be the statesmen that each of you really want to be, deep down on the inside. We the people are ready to put the past foolishness to rest and embark on a fiscally responsible path immediately and beyond any shadow of doubt. If you think about it, we are not responsibly prepared financially for an emergency crisis of any kind. In the event of an earthquake more costly than Hurricane Katrina and 9/11 combined, we'd be in deep trouble. Let's stop beating up on former presidents and simply, honestly learn from their mistakes and get on with the business of fixing the mess. Our government has a dirty diaper, let's just change it.

*"It is impossible to bargain collectively
with the government."*[I]
—GEORGE MEANY

*"Meticulous attention should be paid to the
special relationships and obligations of public
servants to the public itself and to the government.
All Government employees should realize that
the process of collective bargaining, as usually
understood, cannot be transplanted into the public
service . . . . Particularly, I want to emphasize
my conviction that militant tactics have no place in
the functions of any organization of Government
employees . . . a strike of public employees
manifests nothing less than an intent on their
part to prevent or obstruct the operations of
Government until their demands are satisfied.
Such action, looking toward the paralysis of
Government by those who have sworn to
support it, is unthinkable and intolerable."*[II]
—FRANKLIN D ROOSEVELT

8

Protecting Government Workers from Bread Lines

Years ago, I had a conversation with my Italian grandma that we grandkids affectionately called "Mummo." I was asking about grandpa, whom we called "Puppo," who had already passed away when we were having this conversation. Puppo had come to America from Italy at age seventeen without his mother and father. He worked in the coal mines in Pennsylvania; he did farming and carpentry work on the side; and had a rich faith in God. I was asking questions about his work in the coal mines when the subject of unions came up. Evidently, at that time, the conditions of the mines were very unsafe and plenty of accidents occurred. Mummo said, "I know that the unions today (which was the late seventies when we were having this conversation in her mobile home) can really be crooked, but when they came into the mines (in the 1930's), they really improved the safety and working conditions for the miners. Unions were organized because the companies and owners of the mines were not being as wise, respectful, and conscientious of their employees as they should have been. Management's lack of integrity and valuing their greatest asset, their employees, created a vacuum that unions filled." I asked Mummo about where the unions got off, and why she often referred to them as "crooked" today. She said, "Well, they kind of became bullies, like management had been." Mummo passed a number of wise, seasoned insights into my life on this particular day. The elderly have so much wisdom to pass on to us if we'll just slow down long enough to be teachable and ask the right questions.

What about unions today? There has been a significant drop in private-sector union membership to below 10 percent. Meanwhile, Senator DeMint points out that many politicians "have promoted unionization of government workers at every level. Today more than half of all union members work for the government. This has contributed to exorbitant salaries and benefit packages that are bankrupting many states."[1] In listening to my grandma, unions began with a mission of protecting workers. However, what is the need that government (public sector) unions are supplying? Is the government acting so abusively toward its labor force that there is a need for unions to protect employees from the government? If that's the case, then government organizations should consult with businesses to understand what they are doing that is causing 90 percent in the private sector to not even join unions. Just the idea of unions for government-related jobs is quite embarrassing and, indeed, a puzzle.

Have many politicians really created laws that force employers and governments to automatically draft union dues from paychecks? "In the twenty-eight 'forced union' states, workers don't have a choice whether to join organized labor. In these states, if a workplace is unionized, workers are forced to join. Union dues are drafted from their paychecks whether they like it or not (and many most certainly do not). Union dues are then used to make political contributions" to the various politicians that support unions.[2] It's quite disturbing to discover these facts about what is going on and how unwise these kinds of policies are to freedom.

I'm not the only one puzzled by government unions. Bob Williams gets to the heart of the matter in an excellent article. He cites President Franklin D. Roosevelt saying, "The process of collective bargaining, as usually understood, cannot be transplanted in the public service."[3] Former AFL-CIO President George Meany also "viewed government unions as unthinkable."[4] Former Mayor Fiorella LaGuardia and President Franklin D. Roosevelt, "opposed collective bargaining by government employees because government employees enjoy market advantages too easily exploited."[5] All of these individuals recognized the fundamental differences between private-sector unions and government unions. For example, private-sector unions must respect their employer's bottom line, whereas government unions don't. Private-sector union leaders negotiate for their benefits, while at the same time recognizing that excesses might cripple the company and cause eventual bankruptcy. Also, private-sector union members on strike lose their wages; management has to be careful about unreasonable demands in regards to pension and retiree health care. Private-sector managers must be cautious about making unwise concessions that might hinder long-term company profitability.

Meanwhile, as Bob Williams points out:

Government unions are not confined by an employer's bottom line. For public employees, the bottom line is the bottom of the taxpayers' pockets. Most government unions would not exist without forced union dues. One of the first things government union leaders bargain for is a "union security" clause, which forces all government employees in the unit to pay for union services as a condition of employment. If a government employee works in a state with a "union security" clause, the individual must pay tribute to the union. Government unions don't bargain with the taxpayers who pay the bills. When teachers go on strike, they pay no penalty when their absences force schools to close. Adding insult to injury to taxpayers, their actions force parents to either take time off work or quickly find someone else to care for their children. Also, unlike private-sector unions, a government union has a natural monopoly over government services. This monopoly gives government union leaders extraordinary power over elected officials. The money the government unions collect in dues helps to elect politicians who support the unions' objectives. Government unions play a major role in electing their management team. In essence, government unions have a seat on both sides of the bargaining table. The U.S. Supreme Court has made it clear that there is no right to collective bargaining. Collective bargaining for government employees makes them "super citizens" and the rest of the taxpayers are relegated to second-class status. When the government entity bargaining with government employees cannot afford the cost of the union demands, the government increases the fringe benefits (i.e., pension) and pushes the costs off to the future. . . . As a result, national unions have become advocates for higher taxes and government expansion, despite the fact that many of their private-sector members oppose these efforts. . . . Government officials can promise pensions and retiree health care benefits that future taxpayers will have to fund. This, in turn, sucks jobs from the private sector by forcing businesses to pay higher taxes. . . . They lobby every level of government for increased spending and higher taxes. Incidentally, there are no studies that show government workers in unionized states provide better service than those in non-unionized states.[6]

It is understandable for everyone to want to earn as much money as possible. For years, I've heard people's comments about their desire to secure a government job because the pay and benefits are so high. However, our government is not in a place of fiscal soundness. There is no competition within the government as there is in the private sector. It is wisdom for the government to implore mathematics and sound reasoning by commonsense comparison of what the free market is able to substantiate as far as pay and benefits. After all, it is the private sector that is actually paying for government jobs. The only competitive measurement for government employees is to thoughtfully evaluate their pay grid in light of a comparable job in the private sector.

"He who is not contented with what he has, would not be contented with what he would like to have. . . . Are you not ashamed of caring so much for the making of money and for fame and prestige, when you neither think nor care about wisdom and truth and the improvement of your soul?"[I]

—SOCRATES

"I love the man that can smile in trouble, that can gather strength from distress, and grow brave by reflection. Tis the business of little minds to shrink, but he whose heart is firm, and whose conscience approves his conduct, will pursue his principles unto death."[II]

—THOMAS PAINE

"For most leaders, humility comes only by wounds suffered from foolish falls."[III]

—DAN B. ALLENDER

"It is not the creation of wealth that is wrong, but the love of money for its own sake."[IV]

—MARGARET THATCHER

9
Greed and Snake Oil vs. Honest Profit

If a business doesn't make a profit, it will soon be out of business, and all the jobs will join the unemployment lines. Every businessperson has the incentive to seek out and find customers that will buy his or her goods or services. Next, they have the incentive to do that business as efficiently and thriftily as possible without sacrificing quality. All of those goals must come together in such a way that the business makes a significant profit. If the business does not save some of those profits for a rainy day and invest in new and better equipment, it may cause them to go out of business. The recipe for success is just plain hard. That's why most new businesses fail in the first five years. The ones that make it are hugely important to the economy. We should all cheer and believe that our nation will flourish with start-up businesses all across the land. The vision and quest to start or maintain a profitable business is using money as a yardstick for service rendered. Honest people create honest, quality products or services and market it in a manner that is "fairly, squarely, by the rules." Their passion and primary motivation are first and foremost for their products, customers, and employees.

They know if they keep their priorities intact, the money will follow in due time. They courageously take a risk, putting their dream of quality, service, and customer first.

Solomon, who by today's standards had an estimated wealth of 100 billion dollars, wrote: "Develop your business first before building your house."[1] When starting a new business, a businessman or woman must guard against letting any initial success go to his or her head. That's visible when the businesspeople take all the profits for their own personal desires instead of wisely saving for the proverbial rainy day and reinvesting profits into growth and capital improvements in the business. The businessperson must keep a level head and not eat up the lion's share of early profits. You will have plenty of time to slowly increase your personal wealth and receive the financial reward for your hard work. Be smart, and instead of allowing for self-aggrandizement to get the best of you, pursue greater levels of excellence and growth in your business. Solomon goes on to say, "Any enterprise is built by wise planning, becomes strong through common sense, and profits wonderfully by keeping abreast of the facts."[2] Too many businesses and families get ruined when common sense and wisdom are not respected. Solomon continues, "Greedy people bring trouble to their families, but the person who can't be paid to do wrong will live."[3] Be one of those wise and intelligent businesspeople or entrepreneurs who are willing to take a daring risk while maintaining a level head of humility.

In reading a biography about Steve Jobs, I was not surprised to see that he never let the money and wealth go to his head and spoil his passion for creating new and innovative products. In fact, he went out of his way to live simply. In his own words:

> I was worth about over $1,000,000 when I was 23 and over $10,000,000 when I was 24, and over $100,000,000 when I was 25, and it wasn't that important because I never did it for the money. You know, my main reaction to this money thing is that it's humorous, all the attention to it, because it's hardly the most insightful or valuable thing that's happened to me. Being the richest man in the cemetery doesn't matter to me. . . . Going to bed at night saying we've done something wonderful . . . that's what matters to me.[4]

That's a perfect example of pursuing excellence and not being preoccupied with money. Let money follow quality and service.

Back to my days of delivering newspapers, as a young boy it was stunning to read while walking from door to door how many people screwed up their lives due to their obsessions with a preoccupation with money. Clearly, some of the most admirable people on the planet are the missionaries who give their lives and talents to serve those who are less fortunate. How about the doctor who gives up a more lucrative opportunity in order to serve a smaller community off of the beaten path to meet a need and serve an area in which the people are less fortunate? These people join the businessmen and women who create great products and services and are rewarded financially for their accomplishments. They create numerous jobs, and they don't need a union to instruct them how to treat what they consider to be their highly valued employees. In spite of their financial successes, they stay small in their own eyes and are not motivated to excessively consume their profits upon their own desires. Rather, they give large sums of money to charitable causes. The final scene of *It's a Wonderful Life* illustrates the spirit and effect of this kind of life as George Bailey's kid brother, Harry, toasts him as "the richest man in town." Potter may have accumulated far more dollars and cents, but George (played by Jimmy Stewart) was actually far richer.

My Uncle Chike (Anthoney) started his work career driving a truck and distributing beverages throughout the valley in central Pennsylvania. Then he took a risk and bought a bowling alley and turned it into a far more profitable destination for families to enjoy. Next, he bought some buses and served a school district in his area. Soon he was buying more buses and taking on more and more schools. There was no way these public and private schools could maintain the quality and profitability with as good of cost as an entrepreneur. Privately held small businessmen will always find a better way to run things than government institutions. They simply have more incentive! Uncle Chike was another who stayed small and humble in his own eyes and never let money rule his life. He set his nephews up with their own pieces of his business, and he did it in a way where they have the maximum incentive to maintain the high standard and reputation he established. Sounds like a pretty wise succession plan to me.

I refer to these illustrations because they are the opposite of the many stories I was reading about in the newspaper I was delivering when I was a youngster. Some people really weird out when they accumulate success, wealth or power. I read stories about successful police officials who dishonestly made deals with criminals. They just couldn't be satisfied with making honest livings and doing their jobs with their eyes on truth and justice. They could have left a legacy of integrity and honesty, but instead they were deceived by short-term gain and ended up doing harm to the very communities they pledged to protect.

The 1973 movie *Serpico* played by Al Pacino illustrates the point. The Italian patrolman Frank Serpico was shot in the face while screaming for backup during a 1971 drug bust. His fellow officers didn't help and even refrained from immediately calling for an ambulance. Frank was hated on the police force because he was trying to expose the dishonesty, corruption, and dishonest accumulation of money that was occurring among his fellow officers. It took a lot of courage to do the right thing, and his whistle-blowing testimony was the centerpiece of the Knapp Commission hearings, which triggered the biggest shakeup in the history of the department. For his own safety, he had to flee the country once he testified, and he didn't return until many years later only to live a monastic life alone in a one-room cabin, without Internet or TV, that he had built in the woods. He still carries bullet fragments lodged just below his brain from the drug shooting; he is deaf in his left ear; and has nerve impairment in his left leg. His life turned inward as he observed what he saw as an ugly American addiction to materialism and media brainwashing.[5]

What makes this and other stories like this so sad is the fact that most of the police officers are honest men and women who put their lives on the line day in and day out. I've had the pleasure of riding with an officer when I was involved in an initiative of community support for our police department. It is a hugely stressful job that should highly motivate every one of us to be thankful for these men and women. Dealing with a family squabble in which a weapon is involved is so difficult and unpredictable. My brother-in-law, a former member of the army special forces, is representative of the kind of quality and integrity within various police departments.

I realize that there are far too many business leaders and people in other professions who let their most primary motivation slip to lesser matters. It ends up giving a bad rap to the greater number that keep first things first. Not only are they great examples to those under their authority, but they're also the type who are the first to give to charitable causes. The use of class warfare and demonizing successful people for not "giving their fair share" fosters a negative attitude in the country. Besides, the top 1 percent pay 36.73 percent of the taxes; the top 5 percent pay 58.66 percent; the top 10 percent pay 70.47 percent; the top 25 percent pay 87.30 percent; and the top 50 percent pay 97.75 percent. The bottom 50 percent pay 2.25 percent.[6] On top of that, according to the *New York Times,* the political "plan to abolish the Bush tax cuts for those making more than $250,000 is expected to bring in merely $0.7 trillion over the next decade, or about 0.4 percent of Gross Domestic Product per year. As a comparison, the Congressional Budget Office estimates that the deficit over the same period is going to be $13 trillion, more than 6 percent of GDP per year."[7] Plus, when you think about it, just like raising taxes in one state contributes to people moving to another state, in the same way, savvy successful people will find overseas investments to defray some of the tax increase. The government will never see much of that money. Class warfare is popular because those who are uneducated are taken in by the rhetoric that pits the so-called "greedy rich" against the poor and unfortunate working man or woman. It sounds so sensitive and tenderhearted, but it preys upon the weakness of people. We need honest and wise politicians that will follow the words of Abraham Lincoln and appeal to the "better angels of our nature."[8]

In my work as a speaker and consultant, I've had the pleasure of watching people grow and blossom in their productivity and effectiveness. Each business and organization is different in its needs and ambitions to grow and improve. For example, one day, I was contacting car dealerships endeavoring to land some new accounts, and I met with a general manager named Jerry. After spending a few minutes going over how we could contribute to his future growth and success, he got up and closed his office door and pulled his chair directly in front of where I was sitting. He leaned forward, and in a hushed tone, he said, "I don't know anybody on my entire sales staff that's not snorting cocaine. If you can help even a percent of these kids, I'll hire you in a heartbeat." I sat back in my chair and asked a number of questions as he filled in the details. Long story short, Jerry hired our services, and we began teaching the group and meeting one-on-one with the men. They were all kids to Jerry, but in reality the range in age was quite significant. I was thrilled with what unfolded.

As they got to know me and listened carefully to what I taught in the group meetings, they started coming to me one at a time and admitting their addiction and how it was hurting their families and their sales. I was simply teaching the concepts that were working with the many other companies I had worked with, and I never implied that any of them had a drug problem. When you give people a positive vision to focus on and break down the steps that it takes to get there, it pulls out the potential within people. Over the weeks I worked with them, the entire dealership took on a whole new attitude. These guys were overjoyed with what was happening in their families and their business. Their business shot up within weeks, and several months after our first meeting, Jerry let me know that their business had maintained a 30-percent increase since I had started. Jerry is one of those good leaders that kept his primary motivation centered on his interest in developing his employees to fulfill their hidden potential. Some of the wives of the men came to me with tears of gratitude in their eyes for how I had impacted their families' home lives and for the higher income their husbands were now bringing home. Once again, I felt like the biggest winner as I watched the results that unfolded. You simply cannot lift another person up to a higher standard of effectiveness and excellence and not feel better yourself.

Over the years, as my schedule allowed, I enjoyed establishing as many clients as I could that weren't able to pay but were in great need of the work I provided. There were dozens of prisoners I had the pleasure of teaching. On one occasion, the warden, Jack, became convinced that I needed to do more than just teach the inmates. He had already required every inmate to go through my teaching, so he decided to require his correctional officers to attend as well. It was always an interesting challenge to try and win over the reluctant ones that didn't want to be there. It would usually take three or four sessions to finally get through to them, but when it happened, it was fun to watch their eyes light up. I have so many memories of people coming up to me on breaks and going through the litany of reasons they didn't want to be there but now were so grateful to the warden mandating their attendance.

The fact remains that the leaders who focus on developing people, whether it be their employees or their customers, are the ones that prosper and flourish. The system of free-enterprise/capitalism creates the atmosphere to establish a system whereby people can be taught to find their place to excel to their full potential as individuals. Impossible dreams can be accomplished when leaders believe in their people, incentivize their work and train them on how to achieve.

"As for money, the relationship between it and effective schools has been studied to death. The unanimous conclusion is that there is no connection between school funding and school performance."[I]
—BROOKINGS INSTITUTION SCHOLARS
JOHN CHUBB AND TERRY MOE, 1990

"Public educators, like Soviet farmers, lack any incentive to produce results, innovate, to be efficient, to make the kinds of difficult changes that private firms operating in a competitive market must make to survive."[II]
—CAROLYN LOCHHEAD

"It's time to admit that public education operates like a planned economy, a bureaucratic system in which everybody's role is spelled out in advance and there are few incentives for innovation and productivity. It's no surprise that our school system doesn't improve: It more resembles the communist economy than our own market economy."[III]
—ALBERT SHANKER
During his time as head of the
American Federation of Teachers

10

Those Stubborn Facts and Stats—American Education

Being a mom or dad is a daunting assignment. When I found out we were going to have a baby, I decided it was time to begin a study of the subject. I went to the bookstore and bought a number of books, one of them being, *How to Multiply Your Baby's Intelligence* by Glenn Doman. The gist of the book is to motivate parents to take advantage of the first six years of their child's life as foundational in developing their intellectual capacity later in life. The idea was to make learning fun and to scatter short deposits of teaching at multiple times throughout the day, always leaving the child wanting and eager for the next installment. So we made hundreds of large-print, homemade books and had a blast teaching our children to read. They loved it and looked forward to the thousands of short segments we did. We created math cards and games, exposed them to bits of intelligence (encyclopedic knowledge), and did all kinds of creative and fun physical-exercise activities. As I discuss the educational system in America, in no way am I placing that responsibility solely on the school system. Education begins in the home.

We homeschooled our son until he was ready to begin his freshman year in high school and our daughter the seventh grade. We chose the public school because parents that we trusted spoke so highly of the school. It was one of two in the entire area that were rated the highest in the various achievement tests. Naturally, we were very interested in parent-teacher conferences so we could get to know their teachers and stay involved in their learning. When you think about the number of young people these precious teachers impact, it's staggering. My son and daughter had some awesome teachers. My son had a teacher who was very difficult, but all the kids loved her and most of them found a way to learn the material she taught. Why? Because they knew she loved them, and she was passionate about the importance of her subject. That's why she created a high standard and expected them to do their very best.

On the other hand, my daughter had a teacher that had a reputation for being completely incapable of actually engaging his students' attention and was outright boring. It was amazing to listen to the kids describe how much worse he was than the teacher they had for the same subject the previous year. My daughter knew me well enough to warn me not to put my "motivator hat" on when I went to the parent-teacher conference and met him. Because of her warning, my wife also had me on a short leash. My daughter assured me that she would be just fine and that if he hadn't altered his performance in the fifteen years he had been teaching, I surely wasn't going to change him. It was good that I was warned and on a leash because I wanted to reach across the table and just shake some common sense into this guy! I did fine for a while, but after listening to ten minutes of his drivel, I couldn't leave without planting some thoughtful seeds into his career. As we walked away, I was waiting for my wife to lower the boom on me, but she just said something like, "You were fine," then paused, chuckled, and added, "I know it could have been worse for him."

When I was in school, I can remember the teachers that got me so excited about the subject that they taught that I couldn't wait to go to class. Unfortunately, they were quite rare. There were others that just couldn't teach or that weren't well prepared; and it was clear that they were just going through the motions. Later, as a parent, it was disturbing when I had a conversation with a principal and was told how difficult it was for him to release or fire a teacher. Upon reading about the hoops he and other principals had to jump through and the restrictions on their leadership, I was shocked. He loved his school and the students and wanted the best for them but felt boxed in and unable to demand excellence from his teachers.

With my experience in business, I couldn't imagine having to settle for mediocrity because of

IF WE DON'T WISE UP AS A COUNTRY, WE'RE GOING TO LOSE IN THE WORLD MARKET OF YOUNG PEOPLE.

red tape blocking me from pursuing excellence. If we don't wise up as a country, we're going to lose in the world market of young people in the same way our car companies couldn't compete in the world market a few years back. Remember, good teachers deserve to be paid more than average or inferior teachers. Like every other profession, they need the incentive to be the best. Ineffective teachers are so overpaid they need to either become more effective or find another career. Just because public-school teachers are paid by the government shouldn't mean that the incentive to excel, improve and be their best is thrown out of the window. Every profession has to allow for creative destruction, or the standard of excellence goes to pot! After all, teacher salaries are due to the tax dollars from the private sector and profit-making businesses; and businesses constantly evaluate performance. If businesses aren't creative and effective in making a profit, then the market-place fires them. If teachers aren't engaging and effectively teaching students, then principals need to have the freedom to replace them. How do we know they're being effective? Are they producing students that are measuring up against the world marketplace of other students?

I've had the joy of going into public schools and volunteering my services to teach special seminar courses to students. It would happen when teachers or principals would hear me speak or attend one of my business seminars and ask me to teach some of the concepts in their schools. Once invited, my goal was to always find a way to make that connection with some of the more hardened and negative students. I would teach principles relating to goal setting, hard work, motivation and the right mental attitude. I gave the scientific, philosophical and psychological logic and reasoning that coincided with age-old truths. The teachers and their students loved it. Why? I cheated. I asked for divine intervention before I ever left my house.

A study by Harvard University revealed that 85% of the reasons for success, accomplishments, promotions, etc., were because of our attitudes and only 15% because of our technical expertise . . . . William James, the father of American psychology, stated that the most important discovery of our time is that we can alter our lives by altering our attitudes."[1]

If you have a genuine attitude of love, appreciation and respect for people, they intuitively know it. I simply said what the kids needed to hear that would hugely benefit their lives if they applied it. I talked to them about their attitudes and gave them my best sales pitch on how much a good attitude would change their lives for the better. Incidentally, I've had a huge number of kids over the years, as they've grown older, come up to me and thank me for how much my little talks have altered their lives for the better. From teams I've coached, to the various schools I've addressed, the students have responded with the heart of a champion. Kids are always open to adults that sincerely and authentically believe in them as people and that care about them succeeding in their lives. As adults, let's ask ourselves how much we genuinely love, respect and accurately teach kids.

Concerning the importance of teachers, Bill and Melinda Gates and their foundation's research shows that:

> Of all the variables under a school's control, the single most decisive factor in student achievement is excellent teaching. It's astonishing what great teachers can do for their students. Unfortunately, compared to the countries that outperform us in education, we do very little to measure, develop, and reward excellent teaching. We need to build exceptional teacher personnel systems that identify great teaching, reward it, and help every teacher get better. It's the one thing we've been missing, and it can turn our schools around.[2]

At this point in Bill and Melinda's life, they have a great passion to find needs and sound the alarm to alert us of problems, along with finding ways to financially give to various causes. Certainly in this case, we need to pay attention to their findings.

Stanford University's Hoover Institution confirms what the Gates found,

Studies examining data from a wide range of states and school districts have found extraordinarily consistent results about the importance of differences in teacher effectiveness. The research has focused on how much learning goes on in different classrooms. The results would not surprise any parent. The teacher matters a lot, and there are big differences among teachers. What would surprise many parents is the magnitude of the impact of a good or bad teacher. My analysis indicates that a year with a teacher in the top 15 percent for performance (based on student achievement) can move an average student from the middle of the distribution (the 50th percentile) to the 58th percentile or more. But that implies that a year with a teacher in the bottom 15 percent can push the same child below the 42nd percentile . . . . Obviously, a string of good teachers, or a string of bad teachers, can dramatically change the schooling path of a child . . . . The results apply to suburban schools and rural schools, as well as schools serving our disadvantaged population.[3]

This information must serve as a wake-up call. Not only are we strapping our young people with a huge debt load in their future, but we're also handicapping their earning power. The study also points out, "By conservative estimates, the teacher in the top 15 percent of quality can, in one year, add more than $20,000 to a student's lifetime earnings,"[4] which means that those students will earn 13-20 percent more than the average student! Terrific teachers are enormously valuable to our country. It would be wise to encourage and even require principals to steer the bottom 15 percent of teachers onto new career paths. Then, we need to work like the dickens to raise the bar and the standards of the middle 40 percent of the teachers.

Why are these truths flying under the radar? Parents don't know how to interpret the achievement tests that reveal how their kids are being impacted. According to the study, "the teachers' unions have . . . conducted a campaign to convince people that these scores do not really matter very much. Here they are flatly contradicted by the evidence."[5] Who is right? Are Bill and Melinda Gates and the Stanford research correct or are the teachers' unions? It is important to distinguish between the quality teachers and principals that serve in the classrooms from the NEA and the teacher's unions that get all the press. Be that as it may, what are the achievement tests actually showing?

Have you ever heard of the PISA Test? It stands for Programme for International Student Assessment, which the OECD (Organization for Economic Co-operation and Development) gives every three years to fifteen-year-old students in several industrial countries. Its purpose is to determine how they are being prepared for future jobs by having them "use their knowledge of math and science to solve real world problems and to use their reading skills to 'construct, extend and reflect on the meaning of what they have read.'"[6] It appears to be a better way to test a kid's ability to think instead of some of the other rigid achievement tests. So what happened in the latest test in 2009?

America finished just fine if you consider out of thirty-three countries, it was tied for last place in math, twenty-third place in science and seventeenth place in reading as stellar performances! Would a USA Olympic athlete be content with a finish like that in world competition after winning the USA Olympic trials? I have a sneaking suspicion they'd chalk it up as experience and determine to return in four years and come home with a medal. Imagine a professional sports team being pleased with that kind of a finish. As far as that goes, imagine a sports team at any level being happy with that performance against their competition. May I suggest that these scores reveal the need for an even more important mission for our country than the finish of any athletic team, and I'm a big fan of the value of sports in schools?

Who won this competition in 2009 in all three categories? The answer is Shanghai-China. I'm a little puzzled at the results in Shanghai since there are other areas of China that scored differently. Why not combine the entire country like everyone else did? Regardless of China's methods, when you evaluate the USA compared to all the various countries, the results are disturbing. For example, in math we finished tied for last place with Ireland and Portugal. I guess that makes sense when you consider that each of the three of those country's governments are under the strain of financial difficulty. Perhaps there is also a problem with the utilization of math skills with some of the lawmakers within the three governments. The results for math, in order from the top, were Singapore, Hong Kong-China, Korea, Chinese Taipei, Finland, Liechtenstein, Switzerland, Japan, Canada, Netherlands, Macao-China, New Zealand, Belgium, Australia, Germany, Estonia, Iceland, Denmark, Slovenia, Norway, France, Slovak Republic, Austria, Poland, Sweden, Czech Republic, United Kingdom, Hungary, Luxembourg, and then the last three. We were 113 points away from the winning country.

In science, the order after Shanghai-China, down to where the USA finished, was Finland, Hong Kong-China, Singapore, Japan, Korea, New Zealand, Canada, Estonia, Australia, Netherlands, Chinese Taipei, Germany, Liechtenstein, Switzerland, United Kingdom, Slovenia, Macao-China, Poland, Ireland, Belgium, Hungary and then the United States, sixty-one points away from the winner.

In reading, the order after Shanghai-China, down to the USA, was Korea, Finland, Hong Kong-China,

Singapore, Canada, New Zealand, Japan, Australia, Netherlands, Belgium, Norway, Estonia, Switzerland, Poland, Iceland and the United States, fifty-six points away from the winner.[7] Concerning Shanghai's performance, Chester E. Finn Jr., who served in the Department of Education during the Reagan administration, said, "Wow, I'm stunned, I'm thinking Sputnik . . . I've seen how relentless the Chinese are at accomplishing goals."[8] Susan Engel, director of the teaching program at Williams College writes:

> Too many kids in America go to schools that don't even begin to offer them the hope of getting to average . . . . Too many teachers are not that well educated, not that on fire to be teachers, and not that challenged within the system to be terrific. Such schools often lack any coherent or compelling idea about what a good education consists of, what high schools should emphasize, and how to be really vibrant learning communities.[9]

TALENT IS THE NEW OIL AND JUST LIKE OIL, DEMAND FAR OUTSTRIPS SUPPLY.

Where do we start to create excellence and competitive standards with the world marketplace of future workers? The executive search firm, "Heidrick & Struggles, in partnership with 'The Economist's' intelligence unit, has created a Global Talent Index, ranking different countries, under the motto 'Talent is the new oil and just like oil, demand far outstrips supply."[10]

Is the problem not enough money channeled toward education in our country? Senator Jim DeMint writes, "American taxpayers spend approximately $550 billion a year on K-12 public education; more than any other government program and more per child than any other country spends on education."[11] The OECD identifies that the United State spends more per student, $91,700 in the nine years from age 6 to 15 than any other country, with the exception of Switzerland, who pays slightly more per student. We spend 33 percent more than Finland, who is second from the top in science, third in reading, and sixth in math.[12] John Stossel did some investigative research and writes about American K-12 education:

> Spending has tripled! Why no improvement? Because K-12 education is a virtual government monopoly—and monopolies don't improve.
> In every other sector of the economy, market competition forces providers to improve constantly. It's why most things get better— often cheaper, too (except when government interferes . . . . Those experts have been in charge for years. School reformers call them the 'Blob.' Jeanne Allen of the Center for Education Reform says that attempts to improve the government monopoly have run 'smack into federations, alliances, depart-

ments, councils, boards, commissions, panels, herds, flocks and convoys that make up the education industrial complex, or the Blob. Taken individually, they were frustrating enough, each with its own bureaucracy, but taken as a whole they were (and are) maddening in their resistance to change. Not really a wall—they always talk about change—but more like quicksand, or a tar pit where ideas slowly sink.[15]

Senator Jim DeMint writes:

There is a big difference between supporting taxpayer-funded education and demanding that the federal government and teachers' unions run our schools. . . . I am one of the sponsors of the A-PLUS Act. . . . This legislation would allow states to operate much like charter schools; they could agree to certain standards while still being allowed the flexibility to run their schools the way they want. Federal money would be block-granted to these charter states instead of being divided among multiple programs. If states don't meet federal standards, they would have to return to the federal regimen. . . . Successes in one state would be copied and improved upon by other states. Competition for the best schools would raise the standards for schools throughout the nation . . . . Most states now spend more than $10,000 per year for every child in government schools. Even if only half of this figure—$5000—was given to children as a scholarship to any accredited school, the private sector would explode with innovative choices to meet the needs of a wide variety of students.[14]

A study comparing private-school education to public-school education reveals:

Across time, countries, and outcome measures, private provision of education outshines public provision according to the overwhelming majority of econometric studies . . . . If we want to ascertain the merits of real market reform in education, we must compare genuinely market-like private school systems (which are minimally regulated and are funded, at least in part, directly by parents) with state school monopolies protected from significant market competition (such as the typical US public school system). When we assess the evidence using these more specific criteria . . . there are 59 statistically significant findings of market-like education systems outperforming government monopoly schooling, and only four findings of the reverse, for a ratio of nearly 15 to 1 in favor of free education markets.[15]

By a margin of nine to one, Americans believe parents should have the right to choose their child's school, according to a report released last month by Public Agenda, a research organization based in New York City . . . . The National Center for Education Statistics periodically administers the National Assessment of Educational Progress (NAEP) to test the knowledge and skills of the nation's students in grades 4, 8, and 12. Students in private schools consistently score well above the national average. At all three grades a significantly higher percentage of private school students score at or above the Basic, Proficient, and Advanced levels than public school students.[16]

What is the significant difference between private and public schools? Some conclude that the only reason the results are better is because parents who choose to send their children to private schools have greater means. However,

It turns out that of the 8.5 million families with children in grades K-12 with annual incomes of $75,000 or more (the highest income bracket measured), 85 percent have children only in public schools and 12 percent have children only in private schools. (Three percent have children in both types of schools.)[17]

When you combine the total number of K-12 students in all the income levels, that attend private schools, the difference is only 10 percent.[18] I would have expected the difference to be much larger than it is. There must be something else that's motivating parents to send their kids to private schools. There is a reason why parents choose nine-to-one to have the freedom to choose their child's school.

Plain and simple, parents want their kids to be exposed to the best. They're not interested in the bias of some politically correct, restrictive approach that functions in an environment that has no competitive standard. If private schools don't get the job done, parents will simply find a better private school. We're back to the importance of incentives again! The government-run public schools try to raise the bar by rewarding schools that score better on various achievement tests. However, they end up unwisely defeating the purpose. For example,

> Most private schools do not have to teach to a test. As a result, they can afford to focus on teaching your child how to think, as opposed to teaching her what to think. That's an important concept to understand. In many public schools poor test scores can mean less money for the school, negative publicity and even the chance that a teacher could be reviewed unfavorably. Private schools don't have those pressures of public accountability. They must meet or

usually exceed state curriculum and graduation minimum requirements. But they are accountable only to their clientele. If the school does not achieve the desired results, parents will find a school which does.[19]

The private schools still outperform the public schools in the various standardized tests; they just go about it in a wiser manner. This is accomplished even though the private schools cannot pay the teachers nearly as much as the public schools.

To not assign incentives and reward the better teachers is quite antagonistic to sound reasoning, commonsense logic and wisdom. There are some who will pound the pavement for their version of social justice and maintain that equal pay for all teachers whether or not they're effective is the way to proceed. Isn't it wiser to reward the top-15 percent of teachers more than the middle-40 percent, and for the bottom-15 percent to be guided into another profession? There is simply too much at stake! It's far better to learn that lesson now than to be shocked when our young people slide even further in the worldwide market of students. Of all professions, teachers must have the incentive to produce the highest quality students and

OF ALL PROFESSIONS, TEACHERS MUST HAVE THE INCENTIVE TO PRODUCE THE HIGHEST QUALITY STUDENTS AND BE REWARDED ACCORDING TO AN EFFECTIVE RESULT BOTTOM LINE.

be rewarded according to an effective resultant bottom line.

Another early experience I had of the joy of learning the power of incentives was when I had a paper route as an 8-13-year-old. When I secured a new customer to subscribe to the *Toledo Blade*, I was rewarded. When I gave good service to my customers, I often received tips. Later, it was a bummer when I had the minimum-wage jobs and wasn't rewarded based on my creativity and productivity. When in the hotel business, I preferred the lesser-respected bellboy position than the more highly esteemed front-desk clerk. Each customer was an exciting journey of possibility where I had the chance to be rewarded for my efforts. It was even more fun to get to know customers and give them ideas of good restaurants and things to do in the area. I offered so much outgoing and friendly input, that even the cheapskate husbands would get a kick or frown from their wife if they didn't give a good enough tip. I knew most of the people staying in the hotel, at least by face, and we had a rapport the entire time they were with us.

When I was playing baseball my freshman year at college, I worked at a copper pipe factory on Friday and Saturday nights. I learned quickly that there was an incentive to complete the cutting and trimming of more pipes, creating less waste, and not losing any fingers. Later, when in the commission-sales world, if I didn't reach my income goal by Friday, I was up and at it again on Saturday. Teachers deserve to be rewarded if they go the extra mile to tutor students to make sure they are learning the material. On the other hand, there are the pompous teachers who take pride in flunking or assigning *D*'s to a certain number of students. They are simply too lazy and uncreative to get off of their cocky perch and find a way to get through to as many students as possible. Some of those slower students will end up some day accomplishing more than those who aced all their tests. I realize that some kids are not ready to be motivated no matter what you try, but there are far more that just need their teachers to be more creative and work harder.

I had a public-school teacher in the sixth grade that came over to my house to discuss why I wasn't living up to my potential. He enlightened my parents by showing some of the goofball notes I was passing around during class. My parents loved his initiative, and, of course, they sided with him. He sold my mom, who then strong-armed me into buying a set of *World Book* encyclopedias with my hard-earned paper route money! No matter how accessible encyclopedias are online, I'll never sell those: they have sentimental value. Mr. Johnson was a terrific teacher, and I'll always have a warm feeling about him in my heart. The school may not have rewarded his extra initiative with me, but he ended up getting financially blessed in a roundabout way. Kudos to Mr. Johnson!

"The larger the government, the more our living standards are reduced. We are fortunate as a civilization that the progress of free enterprise generally outpaces the regress of government growth, for, if that were not the case, we would be poorer each year—not just in relative terms, but absolutely poorer too. The market is smart and the government is dumb, and to these attributes do we owe the whole of our economic well-being."[I]
—LEW ROCKWELL

"To the man seeking power the poorest man is the most useful."[II]
—SALLUST

"Free enterprise has done more to reduce poverty than all the government programs dreamed up by Democrats."[III]
—RONALD REAGAN

11

The Rich, Poor, and Unfortunate Folks in the Middle

Congress has "created a system in which 47 percent of Americans pay almost nothing in federal income taxes."[1] In breaking down the number, 23 percent don't pay because of low income, 10 percent are benefits for the elderly, 7 percent are benefits for the working poor and children, and 6 percent are other benefits.[2] The greatest problem shows up when someone in the 47 percent tries to get ahead. I've had a number of the elderly tell me that they have to be very careful how much money they earn in their home-based small business opportunities, or they'll lose other benefits. It has also put the low-income people between a rock and a hard place. Shouldn't we be saluting people's initiative with a system that incentivizes and rewards their hard work? People should always have the incentive to make gradual steps in their personal prosperity while gradually decreasing dependence on the government. Senator Coburn reports:

When those low-income Americans do decide to work, their new income is taxed at incredibly high effective rates because when they start making money, they lose benefits. Instead of being rewarded for making the transition from welfare to work, the government effectively punishes the working poor and gives the fruit of their labor to the others. That is hardly economic justice.[3]

That's where the government can act wisely and respect the dignity of people and devise a system whereby they're motivated to at least try to break loose from government dependency. It's hard to believe that some politicians are seemingly allowing this to continue because it creates a strong base of support, in which "a dependent voter is a dependable vote."[4] I've had conversations with various individuals caught in the welfare cycle and listened to their hearts about the matter. These were dear people who explained to me that it was more advantageous for them to continue on welfare than get the kind of jobs they were most likely to be hired for. These precious people would ask for prayer, feeling like they should get a job but were well aware of the quandary it would put them in. Naturally, I encouraged them to take a risk for the sake of their own dignity and self-respect. Those that did, many obtained some degree of help from their church that would come alongside of them to help when they needed it. The charitable giving of these people is commendable, but it would also be wise if policies were more intelligent within the government in the first place.

I read an account of some interesting experiences that a group faced in their various outreach ministries. It illustrates quite well how misguided government welfare programs can harm the attitudes of the recipients:

> A couple of weeks into the Katrina crisis, I sat in a mess tent with some of our workers. One of them pointed out to me how they could quickly tell which hurricane victims had been living on entitlements and which ones worked for a living. They pointed to a rather small African-American man who they said lost his family and everything he owned. He was obviously dealing with unimaginable grief, but whenever a truck pulled in or there was something to do at the base, he was always one of the first to offer to help and would help, working very hard. There were others there who had suffered unimaginable loss, too, but they too were always ready to help when there was something to be done. It was just their nature. All of these worked for a living. Those who lived on welfare were different. Not only were they outrageously demanding, they would get angry if they were asked to do something, even a small thing. We had high school and college students who volunteered to be there and were working harder than they ever had in their lives for many hours a day. Some of those who

had been on welfare would get in the face of these kids at times, demanding to be served and taken care of, often for things they should easily have been able to do themselves. It seemed that right on our base we had both the best and worst of humanity. One basic contrast separated them—working for a living or living on welfare. Call this profiling, but there is some profiling that everyone does. What we're talking about here is not a racial factor—it's an entitlement factor. The entitlement mentality we have allowed has turned some who might otherwise be some of the best people into some of the worst. The blame for this is squarely on us for allowing our government to do it to them.[5]

Conversing with an African-American pastor friend, I was quite surprised to hear how detrimental welfare expansion was to the unwed-birthrate of African Americans. Senator DeMint identified the statistic, "Before President Johnson's welfare expansion, the unwed-birthrate for African Americans was less than 10 percent. Today, with welfare incentives encouraging out-of-wedlock births, over 70 percent of African-Americans are born out of wedlock."[6] His point was that these policies have done much more harm than good for the African-American community. We both agreed that something needed to be done in the inner cities to help the huge amount of unused talent that was there. We were convinced that churches and synagogues would have far more genuine compassion to make a difference. The right kind of compassionate work done by wise people prepared to teach people how to fish instead of just giving out fish would be useful. We also got to talk about racial profiling and how detrimental it was for minorities.

It was similar to the scene in the movie *Remember the Titans* starring Denzel Washington when Sunshine told his African-American friends they would be treated fine in the restaurant. He was introduced to the prejudice they often had to contend with. I'm wired up in a way in which I always want to go to bat for the underdog, and I believe that kind of disrespect just because of the color of someone's skin is deplorable. Martha Williamson produced a particular show from her TV series *Touched by an Angel* where Monica, played by Roma Downy, was given black skin to experience and relate to what it felt like to be a victim of the kind of prejudice and racial profiling that others had to endure. Tess, played by Della Reese, had to give Monica extra support to endure her ordeal. The episode was quite enlightening in regards to prejudice.

I got to know a traveling speaker that was a Native American who told me the stories of some of the prejudice he and his heritage faced and how hard it was to forgive the "white man." Once he did, he was a beautiful example of the kind of love and service to his fellow man that few people have. Watching the opening ceremony to the Olympics is also an excellent example of the beauty of all the diversity and varying nationalities in which a smile crosses all language barriers. I plead guilty to absolutely loving Martin Luther King, Jr.'s "I Have a Dream" speech. What an outstanding demonstration of heartfelt oratory brilliance!

This is why I get so frustrated at the government's mollycoddling of minorities and the thinking that their condescending monetary handouts are somehow going to help. Sometimes it seems like it's just the behavior of people that feel guilty because they know some are less fortunate, and they want to do something without getting their hands dirty. There was a line in *Remember the Titans* when the coach played by Denzel Washington told the coach played by Will Patton that he wasn't helping the black players by taking them aside after he had been tough on them. Denzel chided Will for not understanding that his excessive concern for their feelings was not what these young black men needed to excel in the real world that they would have to face upon graduation. Government policies often keep minorities in a cycle of dependency by throwing money at circumstances that require far more initiative and wisdom than such temporary quick fixes. It might buy a vote, but it worsens a serious problem. I don't mean to be overly critical and harsh, but I've simply seen the consequences of attempts to solve a very serious problem just by the indiscriminate use of money. Many more minority role models along with non-minority men and women could effectively join forces to provide time, attention and mentoring. No amount of government-imposed policies can substitute for the free-will choice of volunteers that will provide respectful mentoring and education. It's going to take strong and honest voices from successful minority figures that will have the courage to tell it like it is. Any segment of minority within our society must self-regulate and honestly access the problems. Then, the non-minorities cannot act as surrogates that choose feeble, money-focused solutions instead of the harder challenge of marshaling compassionate, wise and private free-enterprise initiatives. Current government plans merely divert attention to demonizing the "rich" and appease non-minority "guilt" for the many stupid and unkind past prejudices that have been displayed. There's a reason why Mother Theresa preferred her donors to actually spend some small amount of volunteering their time and service along with their financial gifts whenever possible.

Here is what is at stake. There are huge numbers of smart, talented young people that are wasting valuable time by not cultivating a successful life. In my opinion, there is as much ill treatment and hateful behavior toward others within their own minority as there is pointed toward the non-minorities. All manner of hate and anger has to be faced and healed. From a business perspective, the country needs all this potential intelligence and talent to pursue excellence within their life and the life of their communities, neighborhoods and the inner cities. The current state of education is such that our country needs all hands on deck to get up to speed and fulfill their potential.

Where are the wise and courageous leaders among us that will tell it like it is and go to work to make a better tomorrow? If this kind of vision is going to be pursued, we the people are going to need to take the matter of electing the right politicians seriously. We need men and women that are far better at solving problems than they are at campaigning. Obviously, they have to get elected to solve the problems, but professional campaigners and career politicians are not in the best interest of the country. In the early days of our republic, all the politicians had other jobs that provided their income. That kept them in touch with reality, budgets and the various plights of small business. As far as the professional campaigners, we need to be spared of the entire general, vague, politically correct, milquetoast TV commercials and sound bites that have no substance. And, please, spare us of constantly saying what your image consultants say is the popular message; that is nothing more than saying anything just to get elected.

> AS LONG AS COMMON SENSE AND LOGIC IS VIOLATED, THE GOVERNMENT DESERVES NO ADDITIONAL TAXES.

If our government doesn't set a responsible example of solving problems within the mathematical confines of a budget, then go home and try to support your family with such irresponsible monetary philosophy. In a sense, why should any taxes be raised or loopholes covered if spending is not going to be cut and brought into mathematical integrity? As long as common sense and logic is violated, the government deserves no additional taxes. The principle of being wise and trustworthy with a little before being entrusted with more is pertinent. In fact, the government should be managed like any intelligent business that maintains ample savings for a rainy day. For example, I teach newlyweds to buy a smaller house than they could afford when both husband and wife were working to prepare for their future children and a wealthier future. Then, we suggest they budget to make double payments on their home to save interest and pay it off sooner.

It's a no-brainer that any additional tax revenue for the government, whether from the rich, broadening the base, or closing loopholes, should all go to paying down the debt, not paying expenses. Taxing the so-called rich even more than we already do—as minimal as that would actually be—wouldn't be so bad if we'd use all the money on paying down the debt. In reality, the government would just spend it. Until the government is run like any intelligent business or wise family, it will tend to be the recipient of a certain amount of scorn and frowns from intelligent men and women. We the people want to be proud of our government because it has such a high standard of integrity and thrift. We want to think of the law-writing body of congress as a model for the highest ethical quality of our rule of law, America the beautiful!

Incidentally, there are multiple ways that sloppy math and excessive spending comes back to bite everyone, just like a hike in taxes. For example, "a tax increase is any policy that transfers wealth from individuals to the state. This can be done through direct-rate increases but also indirectly through financial repression—government-induced inflation and the debasement of currency."[7] If interest rates are raised to normal levels, the interest on our national debt will be huge. However, if they remain low, most Americans' savings will continue to dwindle. The government has put us between a rock and a hard place concerning the value of the dollar and our savings. James Madison said, "History records that the money changers have used every form of abuse, intrigue, deceit, and violent means possible to maintain their control over governments by controlling money and its issuance."[8] Sloppy math and off-the-chart discretionary government expenditures, the Federal Reserve's discretionary monetary policy, and greedy, complicated housing loans through banks and government mortgage lenders Fannie Mae and Freddie Mac have all played their part as money changers.

Senator Jim DeMint points out:

> The federal government is now the nation's largest property owner . . . one-third of America's total landmass. By taxing us, our government "owns" over one-third of the profits of all businesses and more than one-third of the incomes of most working Americans. Washington controls and restricts the development of America's energy resources. Government controls the majority of education and health care services in America. It owns the primary retirement income plan for most Americans (Social Security). And government—through a burdensome regulatory system and direct interventions into the financial markets—effectively controls a significant portion of the nation's economic development and business activity.[9]

How could this actually happen in America? It is as if some controlling, manipulative invisible force of socialism has grown like a cancer throughout our government. The Founding Fathers understood the dangers of excessive centralized power, but today's voters are not so familiar with the lessons of history. James Madison said, "If industry and labour are left to take their own course, they will generally be directed to those objects which are the most productive, and this in a more certain and direct manner than the wisdom of the most enlightened legislature could point out."[10] The general populace is far less suspicious of such centralized power, and they become more susceptible to the utopian promises of government control. Beware of the fact that down through history politicians will use a crisis to exploit citizens' fear and insecurity to draw the masses into a greater dependency on some government program. On the other hand, pay attention to politicians who sound the alarm and alert citizens to de-centralize the excessive centralization of power at the federal level.

"The group consisting of mother, father and child is the main educational agency of mankind."[I]
—MARTIN LUTHER KING, JR.

"State education is a mere contrivance for molding people to be exactly alike one another . . . in proportion as it is efficient and successful, it establishes a despotism over the mind, leading by a natural tendency to one over the body."[II]
—JOHN STUART MILL

"Chaos reigns because we cling desperately to meaningless, obsolete beliefs that no longer address our present needs, yet we are still too confused and terrified to embrace a new vision."[III]
—WILLIAM BENNETT

12

The Super-Sizing of Government Programs

It was the Civil War that caused the federal government to institute the first income tax, a flat tax of 3 percent that was later modified to include a graduated tax. However, Congress later repealed the income tax in 1872.[1] In 1894, Congress again enacted an income tax, this time it was 2 percent.

But the tax was immediately struck down by a 5-4 decision of the Supreme Court. This new interpretation by the Court—that an income tax was unconstitutional—created an obstacle for a growing European-style "enlightened" progressive movement in America. Progressives knew that centralized, so-called progressive policies would fail unless the federal government had the ability to tax personal income and business profits. The Founders intended for size and power of the American government to be limited. To be more like the Europeans, progressives knew it must be virtually unlimited.[2]

Nevertheless the progressive dream of unrestrained federal spending was accomplished in 1913 with the Sixteenth Amendment to the Constitution. Initially, due to "generous exemptions and deductions, less than 1 percent of the population paid income taxes at the rate of only 1 percent of net income. This document . . . effected dramatic changes in the American way of life."[3]

Those who proposed the tax, promised it would never exceed 1 or 2 percent, but as Senator Jim DeMint says:

> As is typically the case with politicians' promises, this soon changed. It wasn't long before Congress began to raise taxes on businesses and upper-income workers. This kept the political backlash to a minimum, since most workers did not see their taxes increase. This practice also gave birth to the often immoral and duplicitous use of class warfare strategies employed ad nauseam by progressives who pit different segments of society against each other for their own political gain. Sadly, this rhetoric continues to be front and center in so many political debates today.[4]

Fox News™ legal analyst Andrew Napolitano explains how President Woodrow Wilson, America's first progressive president, has contributed to our current economic crisis as it relates to the abuses of the Federal Reserve. As mentioned earlier in this book:

> The Constitution states that the Congress shall coin money and determine the value of it. For the first 125 years of the nation, that's what the Congress did. But Wilson persuaded Congress . . . to give that power away to a private bank— the Federal Reserve; thereby letting the bankers who ran it, not Congress and not the free market, determine the value of money. And these bankers, who became fabulously rich by doing this, appealed to the weakness in every president . . . free money.[5]

Since that time "The federal government has never been out of debt and has never wanted to be. Prior to the Wilson era, when the government borrowed money, it paid it back . . . . But free money is what Wilson left to his successors, and they all were seduced by it."[6]

The crisis of the Great Depression and World War II provided the seedbed for President Franklin D. Roosevelt to move America more toward European social policies. FDR expanded the power of unions, which are synonymous with centralized power, and he "created a permanent alliance between union bosses and the Democratic Party at the expense of American taxpayers."[7] Under FDR's New Deal, the centralization of the Federal Government swelled due to expanded welfare programs for the poor along with Social Security, which was set up to be a safety net for the elderly that were poor. The workforce paid 1 percent of the first $3,000 of a worker's salary with a maximum of $30 per year. Today, Social Security is 12.4 percent of the first $106,800 of a person's wages. Sadly, today, the government puts the money in the General Fund instead of a Social Security Trust Fund where it belongs. The federal government has borrowed over 2 trillion from Social Security to spend on other programs. Senator DeMint points out, "Contrary to what many Americans believe and what progressives love to say, there is no money in the Trust Fund to pay future benefits. Furthermore, the fundamentally flawed program faces a severe demographic crisis as members of the baby boom generation begin to retire."[8]

FDR ordered a bank holiday so there would not be a run on the bank, and then he required everyone to deliver all gold coin, gold bullion and gold certificates to the Federal Reserve for the price of $20.67 per ounce. Why? Since 1879, the nation was on the gold standard, and the bank failures in the Depression caused the public to want to save their gold. This law gave the government $300 million of gold coin and $470 million of gold certificates. In 1934, the government increased the price of gold to $35 per ounce, which increased the gold on the Federal Reserve's balance sheets by 69 percent. Naturally, these steps enabled the Federal Reserve to inflate the money supply. The government maintained the price of gold at the $35 per ounce until August 15, 1971, when President Nixon declared that the United States would no longer exchange dollars to gold at a fixed value, which was completely abandoning the gold standard. In 1974, President Ford signed legislation that permitted Americans to at least own gold bullion.[9]

Some of the government departments added since FDR were the Department of Transportation under President Eisenhower funded by 18 cents from every gallon of gasoline and regulated the construction of bridges and roads, yet we keep hearing how our infrastructure is deteriorating, which seems to indicate that the amount of money allocated to the government doesn't translate in positive results. Then, President Johnson created Medicare and further expanded welfare programs in his Great Society. Next, President Nixon, created the Environmental Protection Agency (EPA) to reduce pollution to our air and water, but like every other government agency, it ended up expanding far beyond its original mission. It now imposes regulations on nearly every business sector and bases policies on worst-possible scenarios instead of reality. It ends up costing hundreds of jobs and billions of dollars each year.[10]

The Department of Education was created under President Carter to centralize public education in Washington. We've already discussed this issue. Senator DeMint confirms, "At the time, American students were the best and brightest in the world. Today, Americans spend more on education than any other nation, and our students are near the bottom when compared with the rest of the world."[11] As has already been pointed out, the federal government has made things worse, not better. I will say they have made quite a sales pitch when you consider how high the bill has been to lower the actual effectiveness of the end results. I guess we can conclude that they have been amazing marketers to dupe the country for over fifty years.

Joe Kernan and his young daughter, Blake, wrote a book entitled, *Your Teacher Said What?!* Joe is one of the hosts of CNBCs *Squawk Box.* One day his daughter said, "My teacher says the recession is the banks' fault."

Joe responded, "That's way too simple, Blake. For something as big as this recession, there's a lot of blame to go around."

Blake answered back, "And my teacher says it's 'cause we care too much about buying stuff, and it might not be so bad if we stopped."

Joe came back with, "Your teacher said . . . What?!"[12]

This began a journey for father and daughter to understand free-enterprise/capitalism. Joe talks about the values he and his wife want to impart on their children, "We wanted our kids to believe in God, love their country, and respect the principles of hard work and fairness. We wanted them to value honesty, courage, and kindness, to be polite and respectful."[13]

When Blake was nine, her answers told Joe that she had already absorbed a distorted view of economics—from her school, pop culture . . . and just about everywhere else. She was learning that capitalism is unavoidably immoral . . . that businesspeople can't be trusted . . . and that no matter how bad things get, the government will always bail us out . . . he was outraged and determined to do something about it. If he couldn't fix our education system or Hollywood, at least he could teach Blake how capitalism really works, and why it's worth defending.[14]

That amplifies the statement by President Reagan, "Freedom is never more than one generation away from extinction. We didn't pass it to our children in the bloodstream. It must be fought for, protected, and handed on for them."[15]

Parents must first understand free-enterprise/ capitalism before they can pass it on to their children. Our children need to be prepared so they will clearly recognize progressive or statist values that may be pushed by some educators when they attend public schools. Bill O'Reilly, two-time Emmy award winner for excellence in reporting, with Fox News™, points out:

This is a strategy—mentally separate children from their parents—that has been practiced by totalitarian governments all throughout history. In Nazi Germany, there was the Hitler youth. Chairman Mao created the Children's Corps in Red China. Stalin and Castro rewarded children who spied on their parents. That's the blueprint. If you want to change a country's culture and traditions, children must first abandon them and embrace a new vision. Hello, secular progressivism in the USA.[16]

For example, in Los Angeles, students ages seven to ten were given an "educational" survey that asked them to rate how often they thought about, "having sex . . . touching other people's private parts."[17] What is the purpose of such nonsense? As a parent, is this what you want your child's school to be doing? Why not just focus on raising reading, math and science intelligence so our young people can better compete with other countries when they're ready to enter the workforce? Parents tried to get answers, but school officials dodged their inquiries so they took the matter to court. The courts actually ruled against the parents, as Judge Reinhardt, whose wife is the executive director of the ACLU in Southern California, wrote in the unanimous opinion, "Parents are possessed of no constitutional right to prevent the public schools from providing information on that subject to their students in any forum or manner they select."[18] What kind of nonsensical, intellectual baloney is that? As O'Reilly points out, that decision is saying the government can present sexual matters to your child even if you the parent object. Furthermore, it's saying that whatever point of view the school wants to take in regards to sex is acceptable to the courts.[19] In America? That is unconscionable! As Sean Hannity points out, "Too many of our public schools have become liberal indoctrination centers, cultural battlegrounds, and poorly performing graduation factories."[20]

I keep coming back to education because it's so essential to turning our nation in the right direction. It's not only the students but many parents also need to understand what has made our nation great. There are thousands of outstanding teachers and principals that understand and highly value free-enterprise/capitalism and are well aware of the serious stranglehold on public education. They need the help of we the people to alter the landscape of what's going on in our country's educational system. Also, we the people need a grassroots uprising of teachers in order for us to make progress.

Lack of intelligent and correct education tends to be foundational whenever poor or mediocre performance shows up in all fields. Time and time again I've been shocked that companies don't understand the mathematical formula behind long-term success in selling their products or services. Because of their unawareness, they continually have to deal with employee turnover. One of my clients, Gary, managed a real-estate company. After working with and teaching his agents, he wrote to me, "The production of the people . . . is already on a dramatic upswing. Their whole attitude profiles are changing. They are happier, more confident and are spending more time in the field prospecting . . . . they are writing up more business on the listing and sales boards." Sales people quit on themselves due to their fear of failure. It's their fear that keeps them from "failing" their way to success.   In other words, you have to endure many more "no's and rejections" in order to succeed.   It's wise to simply repeat basic principles and fundamentals over and over. They get caught up in looking for the latest and newest discretionary idea that simply diverts them away from the basics. I've always found that I have to first persuade them with many illustrations from every conceivable angle on why persisting with the fundamentals is the key. But it's worth the effort when Roy, a grocery store manager, applies the teaching and tells you he has received three promotions and a 108-percent increase in salary in less than three years.

Incidentally, after a successful career in real estate, Gary and his wife, Sue, took the principles they had learned and started a ministry that ended up reaching around the world with its influence. They took those initial truths they had learned in those teaching sessions and fine-tuned them in a way that impacted thousands of people. He often tells me it's all my fault that he's influenced so many changed lives. I just smile and know that it's another one of those examples of a person taking enduring truths that never fail when they're persisted with until they produce.

One of my key mentors, Zig Ziglar, used to say, "Einstein pointed out that incorrect input requires eleven or more correct inputs to negate the erroneous information. This is another way of saying that it takes a number of 'right thinking' deposits to overcome those stinkin' thinkin' deposits."[21] Herein lies the problem with our country's mistaken ideas about free-enterprise/capitalism. Too many wrong inputs have tainted their views and sullied their minds about the subject. Think about how many movies you have seen that focus on the darkest and most dishonest, crooked and greedy businessmen in society. Obviously, those people are out there, but there are ten times more honest businesspeople that are plugging away day in and day out to deliver the greatest prosperity and standard of living the world has ever known. It's going to take an enormous number of correct and positive inputs to nullify all the negative. We need to start before it's too late.

*"It's better in fact to be guilty of manslaughter
than of fraud about what is fair and just."[I]*
—PLATO

*"The guest will judge better of
a feast than the cook."[II]*
—ARISTOTLE

"Being good is easy, what is difficult is being just."[III]
—VICTOR HUGO

*"When he speaketh fair, believe him not:
for there are seven abominations in his heart."[IV]*
—SOLOMON

*"Wherever is found what is called a paternal
government, there is found state education. It has
been discovered that the best way to insure implicit
obedience is to commence tyranny in nursery."[V]*
—BENJAMIN DISRAELI, BRITISH PRIME MINISTER

13

Restoring Dignity and Self-Respect to the Low Income—Real Fairness

The word fairness is often used when a person is trying to make his or her case, be it right or wrong, logical or illogical, reasonable or unreasonable, true or false. Is it fair for one person to be born with a high IQ and another to be born with a low IQ? Is it fair to be born into poverty while another is born into great wealth? Is it fair for one to be born amazingly attractive while another is the polar opposite? Is it fair to be among the 925 million people in the world that deal with matters relating to hunger every day? That is 13.1 percent or 1-in-7. Of these starving people, 578 million are in Asia, 239 million in Sub-Saharan Africa, 53 million in Latin America and the Caribbean, 37 million in the Near or Middle East and 19 million in the developed countries. Yet, the world produces enough food to feed everyone.[1] Then why hasn't the problem been solved? Before answering that question, let's get back to whether or not it's fair. Many of us have been born and lived in America where having enough to eat is not our primary concern. Why?

Is life fair? I've noticed that life is plain and honest. Yet life doesn't always seem to be unbiased and impartial. All these words are used to contribute to the dictionary meaning of the word *fair*. One thing is certain. Life is what it is. Everyone is dealt a particular individual hand. Our responsibility is to make the best with the hand we've been dealt. Roger Goodell, NFL Commissioner, while fielding questions on the mistaken calls by referees, said, "Sport is imperfect, officiating is imperfect, life is imperfect. That's why I think we all love sports."[2] Isn't it the competition and the incentive to take a risk and see what happens that makes life exciting? Part of that responsibility of making the best of the hand we've been dealt is to realize that "unto whomsoever much is given, of him shall be much required."[3] Whenever tempted to whine and complain about the hand dealt to you, stop right there and take inventory of all the good you have that you're taking for granted. Then lift up your eyes and see the huge need in the world, and ask yourself what you're going to do about it. What you can do comes full circle to why the world is creating enough food, but 925 million are going to bed hungry.

Earlier in the book, I quoted from the book *Why Nations Fail*. The authors write, "If you went back fifty years . . . Singapore and South Korea would not be among the richest countries, and there would be several different countries in the bottom thirty."[4] The authors explain that nations don't fail economically and run into difficulty feeding themselves due to geography. Obviously, geography doesn't explain why South Korea prospers while North Korea doesn't, nor does it explain the differences between north and south Nogales. It doesn't explain the differences between East and West Germany before the fall of the Berlin Wall. History illustrates that countries are not poor due to their climate, geography or culture. The authors identify that "poor countries are poor because those who have power make choices that create poverty. They get it wrong not by mistake or ignorance but on purpose . . . achieving prosperity depends on solving some basic political problems."[5] Simply said, some governments create a political environment that concentrates power in the hands of a narrow elite. This elite governing body extracts resources from the rest of the populace. The government swells in its power while fewer and fewer people prosper. The wiser governments establish political policies that spread power broadly. Meanwhile, these wise leaders uproot the policies that seize the resources of the many and erect entry barriers for new businesses to take a risk. These wise leaders will go out of their way to make sure nothing suppresses the functioning of markets so that only a few benefit.

Many speeches are given by various politicians that use phrases like everyone "paying their fair share" of taxes or a greater amount of "fairness" in our tax code. These statements can tend to sound right. It's implied that the "rich" are living high on the hog at the expense of the little guy who is barely getting by. It's an appeal to our sense of justice.

However, what if these kinds of political policies have never worked in any country or in any government ever in the history of the world. In other words, the "fair"-sounding speeches have never ever actually delivered on their promises of more wealth to the lowest earners and the lowest parts of the middle class. Is it still "fair" to establish polices that hurt the people who need it most? May I suggest that what sounds so fair and just is actually unfair and unjust?

I admit that I wish there were more chairmen and CEOs that were such wise and effective leaders that they would be more preoccupied by the personal fulfillment of creating a profitable and successful business than their compensation packages. It seems to me that creating a culture in which everyone under their leadership is more motivated by excellence and having a servant-oriented corporate mindset is a reward in and of itself. The leader's example creates the vision. The troops will readily follow the stellar example of a wise leader. Money and profits follow keeping first things first. Besides, after a certain amount of money and wealth, isn't it all about creating and leaving a legacy? Why not make that legacy be one that is easier for all employees to respect the example and lifestyle of the leader? I say I wish there were more, but there are many who have that kind of sacrificial mindset. I've had the pleasure of working with many of these leaders in my consulting and other positions of leadership.

One example comes to mind. Most of my involvement with Tom has been one-on-one consultations in which I share key truths and watch him apply those truths in the trenches of his marketplace. Just as I had expected, as so often happens with my connections, I end up learning as much from them as they do from me. Many follow-up conversations took place between us, and he meditated on the truths and made them central to his vision of leadership. Great leaders are passionate about their vision, and they are quick to identify anything that they perceive as less than a person's absolute best. It's kind of like Vince Lombardi's players saying that they like Coach Lombardi far better after practice, after a winning game and after a championship season than they did when they were in the trough and having to deal with his fetishes for quality and excellence. Tom built great teams and enjoyed much success as President of Global Customer Teams for Proctor and Gamble™. After retiring from that career, he created a business that ended up employing around eighty people. For five years, he did not take a salary even though he averaged twelve-hour days. Therefore, it wasn't unusual that his top executive and understudy invested his time and energy to an even greater degree. What motivated Tom and his top executive was building a successful and profitable business. Clearly, a leader doesn't pass up a salary if his primary motivation is money. Yet, his passion and hard work created jobs for eighty people. Tom brightens up when he talks about the growth of one of his employees or some of the work of the various charitable causes he gives to. This is yet another example of the many small businesses that dot the landscape of America the beautiful.

THE LAST THING AN ELECTED OFFICIAL SHOULD DO IS HANDICAP SMALL BUSINESSES AND ENTREPRENEURS WITH EXCESSIVE REGULATIONS AND TAXES.

The last thing an elected official should do is handicap people like this with excessive regulations and taxes. These private-sector jobs create income for eighty tax-paying families that contribute to paying school teachers, firefighters, policemen, the armed forces and, of course, politicians. In my conversations with Tom, his delight revolves around his desire for the employees to succeed and flourish due to the company becoming more and more profitable. Some of those leadership principles that mean the most to him revolve around humility and not thinking more highly of himself than he ought to think. He sees leadership as a role, not an entitlement.

There will always be leaders that are more caught up in their stuff, status, and lifestyle; but we can't let them cause politicians to establish policies that end up handicapping the rest of the entrepreneurs. Life is not fair in that there will always be the poor among us along with the out-of-balance, unwise leaders. We might as well realize that fact and establish political policies that have a proven track record of creating the greatest amount of overall prosperity. We need these risk-taking, gutsy, revolutionary monomaniacs that are willing to go after their dreams. If their dreams make it, the whole country wins. Politicians must remove the obstacles that rob these people of the incentive to make something great happen.

Speaking of monomaniacs on a mission, have you ever heard of Muhammad Yunus's *Banker to the Poor?* As a college professor in Bangladesh, Muhammad became weary of talking about lofty intellectual theories while people were starving across the street. It was 1974, and the country was in a severe famine. He writes:

> The starving people did not chant any slogans. They did not demand anything from us well-fed city folk. They simply lay down very quietly on our doorsteps and waited to die. . . . In this world of plenty, a tiny baby, who does not yet understand the mystery of the world, is allowed to cry and cry and finally fall asleep without the milk she needs to survive. The next day she may not have the strength to continue living.[6]

He committed himself to understand the life of a single poor person. He tried many things to help; some ideas worked while others didn't. "One idea that worked well was to offer people tiny loans for self-employment. These loans provided a starting point for cottage industries and other income-generating activities that used the skills the borrowers already had. I never imagined that my micro-lending program would be the basis for a nationwide 'bank for the poor' serving 2.5 million people."[7]

Yunus got his PhD in the United States, and I was pleased to read that we both shared a fondness for the silly sitcoms *Gilligan's Island* and *Hogan's Heroes.* When he returned to Bangladesh upon graduating, he started his career as a professor. Initially, he felt a thrill teaching his elegant economic theories that would supposedly solve the problems of society. Soon he began to dread his own lectures due to the poverty all around him. When he decided to really seek to understand the plight of the poor, he met Sufiya who was twenty-one years old, had three children and made bamboo stools. She had to borrow 22 cents a day from a moneylender or middleman to buy her bamboo, and then she worked a twelve-hour day making her stools. Then she had to sell her stools back to the middleman to pay for the day's loan. She only made a 2-cent profit after repaying the loan. She and her kids barely survived and were condemned to follow in her footsteps as she had followed in her parents before her. Yanus had the wisdom to realize that just reaching into his pocket and giving her 22 cents was not addressing the problem on a perma-nent basis. Her life was essentially one of bonded labor or slavery. The usurious rates have become so standardized and socially acceptable in Third World countries that the borrower seldom realizes how badly he or she is being oppressed.

As Yanus investigated the situation further, he found forty-two other hardworking poor people like Sufiya who were barely surviving under their money-lenders. This was how he started as a banker to the poor. He loaned 27 dollars to forty-two hardworking entrepreneurs so they could repay the moneylenders and sell their goods in the market at a fair price. As he expanded, it was quite difficult to convince a bank to get involved, but after six months, they finally agreed as long as he was the guarantor. Years later, various individuals in the United States became interested in his work. For example, he met with a group of Native Americans who wanted to supply credit within their communities, so he met with a group of twenty poor Cherokee women. After making his presentation, one woman spoke up, "I have a neighbor who I think could use some money . . . to buy himself a little stove on wheels so he can sell tacos."[8] Soon another woman made her appeal to raise and sell puppies. She felt she could make her idea work with 500 dollars for the first litter. Then there was another who wanted to grow and then sell potted plants. Yunus writes:

> To my great surprise, the repayment of loans by people who borrow without collateral has proven to be much better than those whose borrowing are secured by assets. Indeed, more than 98 percent of our loans are repaid. The

poor know that this credit is their only opportunity to break out of poverty. They do not have any cushion whatsoever to fall back on. If they fall afoul of this one loan, they will have lost their one and only chance to get out of the rut.[9]

Eventually, in 2006, he received the Nobel Peace Prize for his work.

The story of Yunus and his borrowers puts the words *fair* and *fairness* in perspective. Do we do people a favor and treat them with fairness when we redistribute money from the "rich" and give it to the poor with no vision for them to actually apply themselves to get ahead? Deep down inside they have a buried passion and an unused talent to create their own livelihood. They, too, would like to experience a sense of dignity by giving to a charitable cause and paying some small amount of taxes instead of feeling that gnawing frustration of dependency. Don't we treat them with a greater fairness to fan the flames of their own initiative and personal dignity? Granted, there are many who require a little extra mentoring to inspire them to break loose of any habits that are opposite to an ethic of hard work. Perhaps telling them the story of Sufiya will inspire them in their difficulties. One thing is certain about Muhammad's innovative solution to help the poor—it highlights the real meaning of unfairness that's going on in the world. We have to stop wasting time demonizing certain types of people in America the beautiful, such as the so-called "rich." Instead, we should focus on genuine, logical and rational solutions. The problems are great, and there is no time to waste on nonsensical rhetoric.

For example, while discussing what's fair and what isn't, I came across another massive waste of money and time that once again showed up within a department of our government. Public schools and our department of education are at the center of yet another ridiculous misuse of energy and time. Logical, rational, reasonable, fair-minded people will scratch their heads at these cases. "A Vermont kindergartner was forbidden to tell his classmates that God is not dead, because such talk 'was not allowed at school.'"[10] With all the very serious problems in our educational system, what is the purpose of such a massive waste of time? Taxpayer money was spent to defend such nonsense! Why? What subversive harm is this little kid causing? In some other cases, "School administration officials at a Kentucky public school told a student he was not permitted to pray or even mention God at school."[11] "A teacher in an elementary school in Florida overheard two of her students talking about their faith in Jesus and rebuked them, not for talking in class, but for talking about Christ in class. In no uncertain terms, she ordered them not to discuss Jesus at school."[12] As President Ronald Reagan once said, "Christmas can be celebrated in the school room with pine trees, tinsel and reindeers, but there must be no mention of the Man whose birthday is being celebrated. One wonders how a teacher would answer if a student asked why it was called Christmas."[13]

However, it's not just students that are harassed about their natural propensity to talk about matters in their life that they deem important, a "teacher was singled out in a Denver elementary school, where the principal . . . made him remove his personal Bible from his desk, where he kept it to read during silent time. School officials didn't want that book in the students' sight, so they prohibited the teacher from reading it and made him hide it during the school day, even though he never read from it to his students."[14]

In Ohio, thanks to the National Education Association (NEA), teachers who requested that their mandatory union dues be paid to a charity rather than the union's politically liberal causes were annually subjected to an invasive questionnaire. "For years the NEA has issued this particular scheme to intimidate and harass teachers of faith who dare to challenge their radical agenda," said Stephan Gleason, vice president of the National Right to Work Legal Defense Foundation.[15]

Such "politically incorrect" and "rebellious" displays of these students and teachers, run the risk of influencing them to be more dedicated citizens and participants of the school's community, and they could even cause them to be more loving, patient, kind and inspired to teach or do their schoolwork with greater enthusiasm. Wouldn't that be a terrible thing? What if their dedication to their beliefs contributed to the horrendous result of producing the next George Washington Carver or Dr. Ben Carson or other intelligent people that happen to believe in God, the likes of Louis Pasteur or Isaac Newton? Oh my! We must purge the public schools of such future contributors to society! What kind of hyper, nervous, controlling behavior has gotten under the claw of these school officials? It would appear that they need therapy or a support group to talk out their issues in private so that they aren't such a menace to society's respect for good, sound, reasonable behavior.

As a nation, don't we stand for equality of opportunity, not equality of income? Equality of income is not most people's idea of fairness. As a country, in both business and government, it's in the best interest of our ability to compete with other countries to establish incentive whereby we reward hard work and initiative. The other day, I was talking to an electrician who learned his trade as a young man and then acquired self-discipline in the marines. He was telling me that his work ethic was making his peers in the company look bad because he worked three times faster with greater quality than everyone else. Instead of his boss rewarding his initiative and hard work with more money, they merely took him away from the contract he was working on to help his co-workers get caught up on their contracts. That kind of unfairness is foolish to morale! His fellow employees may initially fuss and complain, but wise leadership should always reward the kind of performance that they want to see duplicated. The government must function with the same kind of wisdom. Speed of the leader, speed of the team! You reward what you want to see more of.

MY FRIENDS, SOME YEARS AGO THE FEDERAL GOVERNMENT DECLARED WAR ON POVERTY AND POVERTY WON.

—RONALD REAGAN

Let's get up-to-speed and educate ourselves so that we can recognize what's good for free-enterprise/capitalism. When lofty speeches about fairness dominate the landscape, let's follow the wisdom of a wise sage who said, "Yet with their plausible and attractive arguments they deceive those who are too simple-hearted to see through them."[16] For decades, we've tried worn-out and irresponsible strategies to alleviate poverty. In 1988, President Reagan delivered a State of the Union Address in which he declared, "My friends, some years ago, the Federal Government declared war on poverty, and poverty won."[17] Wouldn't it be interesting if 50 percent of the current money to help the poor was instead channeled to businesses, churches and synagogues to come up with a joint plan without the obstacles of the government, and Muhammad Yunus was brought in as a consultant. Just a thought.

Governments are very limited in what they can provide. Dr. Coburn wisely points out:

The main lesson at the intersection of faith and politics is this: government can do justice, but not charity. Government simply was not designed to do charity. When a free citizen does charity, two people benefit—the person doing the charity and the person receiving the charity. When government does the charity, it creates dependency and denies the individual the benefit of providing charity.[18]

Frederic Bastiat, a French champion of free-enterprise/capitalism, wrote, "Everyone wants to live at the expense of the state. They forget that the state lives at the expense of everyone."[19] Our third president, Thomas Jefferson, wrote, "The republic will cease to exist when government takes from those who are industrious and gives to those who refuse to work."[20] If you've lost your zeal for what has made America great, then find an immigrant that has started a successful business, and listen to them get all teary eyed as they talk about the opportunity in America. Some of us need to really educate ourselves about free enterprise. It's apparent it has become too minimal and unimportant to far too many third and fourth generation Americans. Thomas Paine wrote, "What we obtain too cheap, we esteem too lightly; it is dearness only that gives everything its value."[21] Pass the word; history has taught us that free-enterprise/capitalism is the only path to a more prosperous nation for the poor, the middle class and the rich.

"You can always count on Americans to do the right thing—after they've tried everything else."[I]
—WINSTON CHURCHILL

"An army of principles can penetrate where an army of soldiers cannot."[II]
—THOMAS PAINE

"A decline in courage may be the most striking feature that an outside observer notices in the West today. The Western world has lost its civic courage . . . . Such a decline in courage is particularly noticeable among the ruling and intellectual elite, causing an impression of a loss of courage by the entire society."[III]
—ALEKSANDR SOLZHENITSYN

"America is great because she is good. If America ceases to be good, America will cease to be great."[IV]
—ALEXIS DE TOCQUEVILLE

14

Can America Make a Fourth-Quarter Comeback?

One of the most exciting parts of a football or basketball game is watching the momentum shift as a team, usually led by a gutsy and skillful leader, musters up the energy and timely plays to pull a game out in the waning seconds. It seems like an amazing work of art as we witness these rigorous rallying of the troops. Any thoughtful observer of the plight of America wonders if it's too late to engineer a comeback that will actually cause the fans of America to stand up and cheer. Who will lead such a comeback? Can we find someone gutsy and skillful enough to rally the troops? What would the strategy be? Are we, as the team, able to marshal the courage and outright energy to do what it takes to win?

If we're going to make that comeback, it's going to take lots of grassroots-level individuals that understand the actual facts of what's going on in each of the areas mentioned in this book. Polls can reveal people's current opinion, but only being accurately abreast of the facts enables one to have the right opinion. Steve Jobs was asked by his staff, "Should we do some market research to see what customers want?"

He responded, "No, customers don't know what they want until we've shown them!"[1] It's not an indictment to not know what you want until some informed or creative person is inspired to discover or invent something beyond what you had the capacity to imagine. Many people in America know that our country is facing huge problems, but they have no idea how to solve them. The need for visionary leadership to invent the future, another of Steve Jobs's maxims, has perhaps never been greater. Likewise, most people in America know what they want for themselves, but they don't know what needs to happen in the country to increase the chances of them achieving their personal goals. Once enough people at the grassroots level become informed of the facts and spread the word, this nation can experience a fourth-quarter comeback!

Every problem that I observe in our nation and government comes back to "we the people." Melting it down further, each of us could also humbly admit, "I am part of the problem." If I start with that obvious admission then I'm also assuming the responsibility to do something about the problems. We've just come through another hurricane in the gulf area, another along the east coast, along with the worst draught in fifty years. I'm not saying that time and chance and randomly unpredictable and bad things are never going to happen. These dear farmers will suffer but so will the rest of us, along with the rest of the world that benefits from our good harvests.

Ben Franklin made a plea for prayer at the Constitutional Convention in Philadelphia in 1787:

We have gone back to ancient history for models of Government, and examined the different forms of those Republics which having been formed with the seeds of their own dissolution now no longer exist. And we have viewed Modern States all round Europe, but find none of their Constitutions suitable to our circumstances. In this situation of this Assembly, groping as it were in the dark to find political truth, and scarce able to distinguish it when presented to us, how has it happened, Sir, that we have not hitherto once thought of humbly applying to the Father of lights to illuminate our understandings? In the beginning of the Contest with G. Britain, when we were sensible of danger we had daily prayer in this room for the divine protection. Our prayers, Sir, were heard, and they were graciously answered. All of us who were engaged in the struggle must have observed frequent instances of a Superintending providence in our favor. To that kind providence we owe this happy opportunity of consulting in peace on the means of establishing our future national felicity. And have we now forgotten that powerful friend? I have lived, Sir, a long time, and the longer I live, the more convincing proofs I see of this truth—that God governs in the affairs of men. And if a sparrow cannot fall to the ground without his notice, is it probable that an empire can rise without his aid? We have been assured, Sir, in the sacred writings, that 'except the Lord build the House they labour in vain that build it.' I firmly believe this; and I also believe that without his concurring aid we shall succeed in this political building no better than the Builders of Babel: We shall be divided by our little partial local interests; our projects will be confounded, and we ourselves shall become a reproach and bye word down to future ages. And what is worse, mankind may hereafter from this unfortunate instance, despair of establishing Governments by Human Wisdom and leave it to chance, war and conquest. I therefore beg leave to move, that henceforth prayers imploring the assistance of Heaven, and its blessings on our deliberations, be held in this Assembly every morning before we proceed to business, and that one or more of the Clergy of the City be requested to officiate in that service.[2]

The humility that Franklin demonstrated is greatly needed among authority figures in our country. There is actually quite a history of presidents that expressed their humility by highly respecting and valuing the Bible. Ponder what some of our greatest presidents say about the Bible. George Washington said, "It is impossible to rightly govern the world without God and Bible."[3] Abraham Lincoln said, "I am busily engaged in the study of the Bible. I believe it is God's word because it finds me where I am. I believe the Bible is the best gift God has ever given to man. All the good of the Savior of the world is communicated to us through the Book."[4] Theodore Roosevelt said, "A thorough understanding of the Bible is better than a college education."[5] He also said, "To every man who faces life with real desire to do his part in everything, I appeal for a study of the Bible."[6] Ronald Reagan said, "Of the many influences that have shaped the United States into a distinctive nation and people, none may be said to be more fundamental and enduring than the Bible."[7] He also observed, "Within the covers of the Bible are the answers for all the problems men face."[8] Thomas Jefferson said, "I have always said and always will say that the studious perusal of the Sacred Volume will make better citizens, better fathers, better husbands . . . the Bible makes the best people in the world."[9] Harry Truman said,

> The fundamental basis of this nation's law was given to Moses on the Mount. The fundamental basis of our Bill of Rights comes from the teaching we get from Exodus and St. Matthew, from Isaiah and St. Paul. I don't think we emphasize that enough these days. If we don't have the proper fundamental moral background, we will

finally end up with a totalitarian government which does not believe in the right for anybody except the state.[10]

Andrew Jackson said, "The Bible is the Rock on which this Republic rests."[11] John Q. Adams said, "My custom is to read four or five chapters of the Bible every morning immediately after rising . . . . It seems to me the most suitable manner of beginning the day . . . . It is an invaluable and inexhaustible mine of knowledge and virtue."[12] Ulysses S. Grant said, "The Bible is the sheet-anchor of our liberties."[13] Herbert Hoover said, "The study of the Bible is a post-graduate course in the richest library of human experience."[14] When you realize the enormous honor that presidents gave this book, it's even more embarrassing when educators and school officials actually harass students and various teachers that also value the same book. It's even more alarming when history tells us that in early American classrooms, this was the book they used to teach kids to read. After all, it is by far the number-one selling book of all time.

Admittedly, it looks quite gloomy on the horizon when you consider the lobbying of elected officials to bring home the bacon. How in the world are we going to transition from a society of "I've got to get mine" to a society of President Kennedy's request, "Ask not what your country will do for you, but what you will do for your country." How will that ever actually happen, short of a miracle? What's the likelihood of large corporations who are desperately trying to protect and grow their revenues and net profits to suddenly stop trying to lobby so as to protect themselves from losing market share to the smaller competitors? These eager young bucks are biting at their heels eagerly trying to capture market share. Why can't we once and for all establish clear-cut, rule-of-law-type policies, that pick zero favorites and let the marketplace determine the winners. If ever we needed the vision of Vince Lombardi, "The object is to win fairly, squarely, by the rules—but to win," it's today! If the rules are not clear and unchangeable, how can one win fairly, squarely and by the rules? It's as if there are nonexistent rules always open for negotiation to the highest lobbying bidder.

Various individuals and groups are desperately trying to keep and hold onto their piece of government pie. It would indeed take a monumental miracle for that self-centered attitude to suddenly change. We certainly can't afford to join Doris Day in singing "Que Sera Sera." For those who have never seen Alfred Hitchcock's movie, *The Man Who Knew Too Much,* Doris Day sings about giving into the idea of fate deciding whatever might happen in the future, instead of an educated and energized populace making it happen.

Another one of my clients, Keith, brought me into his publishing company. We spent every evening for two weeks with all his employees from shipping, to office personnel, editors, artists, marketers and department heads. To this day, he still has people coming up to him and pointing out how their lives changed from that two-weeks on forward. Keith says, "The morale of the whole company went up 100 percent. We had a whole new company. It was the best decision I ever made in business." Keith is another one of those leaders that truly loves his employees and is ready to do whatever it takes to train them to fulfill their potential. His voice comes alive with amazement when he talks about Thelma. She was nine-months pregnant and right at her due date when we started the training. One of the Thursdays had not been scheduled due to previous commitments before the training started. After the first night, Thelma didn't want to miss any sessions by having her baby, so she prayed that she would have her baby on the Thursday when there was no session scheduled. Sure enough, she had her baby on Thursday and was back in class with baby in her lap on Friday.

He also tells of an individual in shipping that said, "Nobody ever told me I could think differently." Another guy in shipping thanked him profusely for "believing in him." After the training, Keith started a reading program in the company. Keith would select a book and buy it for all his employees, and they read one a month and would talk about what they were getting out of it. When one of his employees needed to move after three years working for the company he told him, "I never read before I started working here. I've read thirty-six books in the last three years, and I'm now going to be a reader for the rest of my life." He will be in good company since George Washington said, "I conceive that a knowledge of books is the basis on which all other knowledge rests."[15] Thomas Jefferson said, "I cannot live without books."[16] Theodore Roosevelt said, "I am a part of everything that I have read."[17] Dwight Eisenhower said, "Don't be afraid to go in your library and read every book."[18]

That's the kind of thinking it's going to take to turn our nation in a more positive direction. It's going to take a passion for learning and understanding why free enterprise was so important to our founding fathers that they risked their lives to fight for the freedom to pursue it with minimal government intervention and restriction. Nobody is lessening the good that intelligent and sound government policy can contribute to the nation. Nevertheless, it's the individual patriotism and deep appreciation for free-enterprise/capitalism that will make us be that "shining city upon a hill whose beacon light guides freedom-loving people everywhere."[19] It will require a passion for truth within each of us.

Winston Churchill said, "The truth is incontrovertible. Malice may attack it, ignorance may deride it, but in the end—there it is."[20] When you tell the truth and search for truth, you will remain on solid footing. As that great philosopher Elvis Presley said, "Truth is like the sun. You can shut it out for a time, but it ain't goin' away."[21] Thomas Jefferson said, "It is error alone which needs the support of government. Truth can stand by itself."[22] Naturally, there is no benefit to naively buying into what someone in authority tells you if it can't be substantiated with truth. Albert Einstein said, "Unthinking respect for authority is the greatest enemy of truth."[23] It was right and proper for Dietrich Bonhoeffer to practice civil disobedience when the Nazi party was trying to get a foothold in Germany during World War II. He ended up being shot for speaking out. Let's work hard before our America the beautiful ever gets even the least bit close to we the people having to practice civil disobedience.

As Ronald Reagan said in his farewell address to the nation:

I've spoken of the Shining City all my political life. . . . In my mind it was a tall, proud city built on rocks stronger than oceans, windswept, God-blessed, and teeming with people of all kinds living in harmony and peace; a city with free ports that hummed with commerce and creativity. And if there had to be city walls, the walls had doors and the doors were open to anyone with the will and the heart to get here. That's how I saw it, and see it still.[24]

We may have become weakened, but we are still that shining city upon a hill. I burn with passionate delight when I listen to one of the dozens of public and private school teachers that tell me about their love and interest in their students. These mighty stalwarts in our educational system inspire me about how we can turn our challenges into stars. They go the extra mile to make sure the lights get turned on in their students' eager young minds. I get teary-eyed as I watch them get teary-eyed articulating what motivates them. They talk of staying up late writing extra remarks on their students' papers and then turn around to be there the next day to experience another golden moment to advance another young person's life.

Then there's that seasoned veteran owner of a business that is facing tough times. Their better judgment tells them to cut back their employees, but they hang on as long as they can in hopes of things turning around. Their hearts ache when that day approaches, and they are as pained as the individuals that suddenly find themselves out of work. They vow to regroup and find a way to bounce back in the future. The temporary setbacks of life cause the remaining employees to have to work harder, longer hours and take on additional responsibilities. Those that lost their jobs search and search, while some find another job in his or her field, others have to settle for a less-paying job. Nevertheless, in each case they do what it takes because they're made of scrappy stuff that has made America great. Don't tell me that these kinds of people can't turn this nation upside down to get us back on course! From the young buck of an entrepreneur that ventures out of his comfort zone to take his or her calculated risk to the middle-class college student who couldn't get much financial aid and has to work at a restaurant to pay tuition and board, we are a people who will rise to the occasion and just do it!

Everybody has their dream. In America, that dream can be attempted; and when we fail, we put on the necessary bandages and bounce back to try again from another angle. Why do we do it? Because in America we can! Just like we bounced back as a nation in 1980, we can do it again. We can cause our Founding Fathers to shed their tears as they look over the portals of heaven and see that once again America has righted our wrongs and remained that shining city on a hill.

Notes

Introduction

[1] http://www.globescan.com/news_archives/pipa_market.html.

[2] Ibid.

1 Incentive: What's in It for Me

[1] Quote from Ronald Reagan on http://thinkexist.com/quotes/with/keyword/incentives/.

[11] Thomas Jefferson, First Inaugural, (1801), http://ahp.gatech.edu/jefferson_inaug_1801.html.

[1] Most people credit Abraham Lincoln with this quote. There are some who claim that William Boetcker was responsible for it. Either way, there is great wisdom in these words.

[2] W. Michael Cox and Richard Alm, "Creative Destruction," *Library of Economics and Liberty*, http://econlib.org/library/Enc/CreativeDestruction.html.

[3] Matthew 25:14-30 MSG

[4] Tim Kane, "Press Release: New Study: Startup Job Creation Collapse," *Market Watch: The Wall Street Journal*, (13 September 2012), http://www.marketwatch.com/story/new-study-startup-job-creation-collapses-2012-09-13.

[5] Dr. C. Thomas Anderson, *Will the Real America Please Stand up?*, (Tulsa: Harrison House Publishers, 2011), 167-173.

[6] Zig Ziglar, *See You at the Top*, (Gretna: Pelican Publishing Company, 2006), 359.

[7] Ibid., 359.

[8] Ibid., 361.

⁹ Steven E. Landsburg, *The Armchair Economist: Economics and Everyday Life*, excerpt from chapter 1, *Freedom Keys*, http://freedomkeys.com/pricecontrols2.htm.

¹⁰ Ziglar, *See You at the Top*, 361.

¹¹ Zig Ziglar, *Born to Win: Find Your Success Code*, (Ziglar Success Books, 2012), 63.

¹² Ziglar, *See You at the Top*, 305.

¹³ Dr. Mark J. Perry, "The Two Americas: Public Sector vs. Private Sector," mjperry.blogspot.com/2010/02/two-americas-public-sector-vs-private.

2 How the Gipper Got it Right—Reagan and Today

ᴵ Quote from Ronald Reagan on http://thinkexist.com/quotes/with/keyword/incentives/.

ᴵᴵ Quote from Herbert Hoover http://www.brainyquote.com/quotes/keywords/incentive.

ᴵᴵᴵ Quote from Calvin Coolidge on http://www.quotationcollection.com/tag/free%20enterprise/quotes.

ᴵ Quote by Ronald Reagan on http://www.goodreads.com/author/quotes/3543.Ronald_Reagan.

² Jim DeMint, *Now or Never*, (New York: Hatchette Book Group, 2012) 83.

³ Gerald F. Seib, "How Did Reagan's Economic Headaches Compare?" *The Wall Street Journal*, (22 January 2009).

⁴ Ronald Reagan, "Radio Address to the Nation on Prayer in Schools," (25 February 1984), http://www.presidency.ucsb.edu/ws/index.php?pid=39565.

⁵ Stuart MacPhail, "An Open Letter—To Those Who Yearn For America to Get Its Financial House in Order," bba4usa.org/an_open-letter_BBA.html.

[6] Nikitas3, "About that 'Reagan Debt,'" *RedState*, (25 May 2011), http://wwwredstate.com/nikitas3/2011/05/25/about-that-reagan-debt.

[7] Eric Widdison, "U.S. National Debt & Interest Expense by Presidential Term," *PresidentialDebt.org*, (14 August 2012), http://www.skymachines.com/US-National-Debt-Per-Capita-Percent-of-GDP-and-by-Presidental-Term.htm.

[8] David M Kotz and Fred Weir, *Why Did the Soviet Union Fall?* see "The Revolution from Above" on http://answers.yahoo.com/question/index?qid=20101117175524AAFp7XF.

[9] Widdison, "U.S. National Debt," tp://www.skymachines.com/US-National-Debt-Per-Capita-Percent-of-GDP-and-by-Presidental-Term.htm.

[10] Ibid.

[11] U.S. Inflation Calculato, (measures the buying power of the dollar over time), http://www.usinflationcalculator.com.

[12] Quote from Ronald Reagan on http://www.goodreads.com/author/quotes/3543.Ronald_Reagan.

[13] Quote from Abraham Lincoln on http://www.brainyquote.com/quotes/authors/a/abraham_lincoln.html]

3   How to Screw up a Nation in One Easy Lesson

[I] Quote from Winston Churchill on http://paragonality.com/2012/07/31/some-assorted-winston-churchill-quotes-on-free-enterprise/.

[II] Quote from John Kenneth Galbraith on http://quotationsbook.com/quotes/tag/free_enterprise/.

[III] Quote from Margaret Thatcher on http://listverse.com/2007/12/21/top-25-quotes-of-margaret-thatcher/.

[1] Daron Acemoglu, the Killian Professor of Economics at MIT and winner of the John Bates Clark Medal awarded to economists who have made the most significant contribution to

economic thought and knowledge; and James A. Robinson, a political scientist and an economist who is the David Florence Professor of Government at Harvard University, *Why Nations Fail*, (New York: Crown Publishers, 2012), 75.

2 Ibid., 77.

3 Mark Steyn, *After America—Get Ready for Armageddon*, (Washington, DC: Regnery Publishing, 2011), 106-107.

4 Patricia Reaney, "Washington, D.C.: Favorite Area for the Wealthy Young," *Reuters*, (16 September 2009), cited by Mark Steyn, *After America*, 50.

5 "The Richest Counties in America," *Newsweek*, (10 November 2010), cited by Mark Steyn, *After America*, 51.

6 Zig Ziglar, *Steps to the Top*, (Gretna: Pelican Publishing, 1985), 32.

7 Dr. Robert Coles, author of *The Moral Intelligence of Children*, in an interview with David Gergen, "Basic Humanity," Transcript, (21 February 1997), http://pbs.org/newshour/gergen/february97/coles_2-21.

8 Quotes by George Washington taken from http://sites.google.com/site/byuheroesofhistory/georgewashington.

9 Quote from Winston Churchill taken from *Thinkexist.com*, http://thinkexist.com/quotation/a_vocabulary_of_truth_and_si mplicity_will_be_of/185644.

10 Quote from Niccolo Machiavelli on http://publicquotes.com/source/181/niccoló-machiavelli.html.

11 William Shakespeare, *Hamlet*, Act 2, Scene 2, page 8, http://nfs.sparknotes.com/hamlet/page_100.html.

12 Tamar Frankl, *Trust and Honesty: America's Business Culture at a Crossroads*, (Oxford: Oxford University Press, 2006), 5.

13 Dr. Steven Berglas, "The Top 10 Reasons Lying Will Corrode Your Self-Esteem," *Forbes*, (20 January 2012), http://www.forbes.com/sites/stevenberglas/2012/01/20/the-top-10-reasons-lying-will-corrode-your-self-esteem/.

4 The Borrower Is Servant to the Lender

[I] Quote from Warren Buffett on http://www.miproconsulting. com/blog/2011/07/warren-buffett-incentives/.

[II] Quote from Winston Churchill on http://www.paragonality. com/2012/07/31/some-assorted-winston-churchill-quotes-on-free-enterprise/.

[III] Quote from Alexis de Tocqueville on http://www.goodreads. com/author/quotes/465.Alexis_de_Tocqueville.

[1] George Washington in his farewell address to the nation, http;//www.pbs.org/georgewashington/milestones/farewell_ address_about.html.

[2] Ibid.

[3] Justin Soutar, "The Two-Party System: A Catastrophic Failure," *DinarVets*, (30 August 2007), http://dinarvets.com/forums/ index.php?/topic/116156-the-two-party-system-a-cata-strophic-failure/.

[4] Proverbs 22:7 KJV

[5] Geoff Colvin, senior editor-at-large, *Fortune*, "Adm. Mike Mullen: Debt Is Still Biggest Threat to U.S. Security," (10 May 2012), management.fortune.cnn.com/2012/05/10/admiral-mike-mullen.

[6] Carmen Reinhard and Kenneth Rogoff, *This Time is Different: Eight Centuries of Financial Folly*, cited by U.S. Senator Tom Coburn, M.D., *The Debt Bomb*, (Nashville: Thomas Nelson Inc., 2012), xiii-xiv.

[7] Tom A. Coburn, *The Debt Bomb*, (Nashville: Thomas Nelson, 2012) 12.

[8] "Too Much Debt Means the Economy Can't Grow: Reinhart and Rogoff," *Bloomberg View*, (13 July 2011), cited by Coburn, *The Debt Bomb*, 13.

[9] Rob Bluey, "Federal Government's Debt, Unfunded Obligations Grew Rapidly Last Year," *The Foundry*, (7 June 2011), cited by Coburn, *The Debt Bomb*, 15.

[10] Michael D.Tanner, "Bankrupt: Entitlements and the Federal Budget," CATO Institute Policy Analysis 673, (28 March 2011), cited by Coburn, *The Debt Bomb*, 16.

[11] Jon Ward, "Bernanke Headlines a Day of Grim Warnings About the Nation's Fiscal Standing," *Daily Caller*, (4 February 2011), cited by Coburn, *The Debt Bomb*, 16.

[12] Chris Arnold, "Debt's Impact Could Be Worse If Interest Rates Rise," (22 July 2011), cited by Coburn, *The Debt Bomb*, 20.

[13] Coburn, *The Debt Bomb*, 20.

[14] Marc Labonte, Specialist in Macroeconomic Policy, and Justin Murray, Information Research Specialist, "Foreign Holdings of Federal Debt," *Federation of American Scientists*, (2 July 2012), http://www.fas.org/sgp/crs/misc/RS22331.pdf, 4.

[15] Senator Jim DeMint, *Now or Never*, (New York: Hatchette Book Group, 2012), 21.

[16] Nicole and Mark Crain, U.S. Small Business Administration Office of Advocacy, cited by Jim DeMint, *Now or Never*, 138.

[17] Quote from Ronald Reagan on http://quotedb.com/quotes/3261.

[18] W. Kirk Iddell, president of IREX Corporation reported the study of Manufacturers Alliance/MAPI, (14 July 2011), http://democrats.energycommerce.house.gov/sites/default/fil es/image_uploads/Testimony_CMT_07.14.11_Liddell.pdf, 4.

[19] DeMint, *Now or Never*, 139.

[20] Mark Johanson, *International Business Times*, (2 August 2011), cited by DeMint, *Now or Never*, 140.

[21] Vincent Trivett, "The TRUTH About Who Really Owns All Of America's Debt," *Business Insider*, (20 July 2011), businessinsider.com/who-owns-us-debt-2011-7.

5   Bankers, Gold, and Jekyll Island

[1] Quote from Thomas Jefferson on http://barefootsworld.net/banking-fed-quotes.

Notes

[II] Henry Cabot Lodge, Sr., Ibid.

[III] Charles A. Lindbergh, Sr., Ibid.

[1] Ecclesiastes 1:9 KJV.

[2] "Democrats Failure to Pass Budget Is Illegal," *Investor Business Daily,* (10 February 2012), http://news.investors.com/ibd-editorials/021012-600854-democrats-refusal-to-pass-budget-is-illegal.htm.

[3] *New Oxford American Dictionary,* 2nd ed. Ed. Erin McKean, (New York: Oxford Press, 2005), Also available at oxfordamericandictionary.com.

[4] "What Happened?" *Gold Standard Solution,* http://www.goldstandardsolution.com/what-happened/.

[5] Professor Bernard Corry, "Keynesianism," *New Perspective,* vol. 5, no. 1, http://www.history-ontheweb.co.uk/concepts/keynesianism51.htmontheweb.co.uk/concepts/keynesianism51.

6 Money Madness = $16 Trillion and Climbing

[1] George Washington to Jabez Bowen, Rhode Island, (9 January 1787), http://barefootsworld.net/banking-fed-quotes.

[II] Quote from Barry Goldwater, (ran for president in 1964), on http://barefootsworld.net/banking-fed-quotes.

[III] Henry Ford, Ibid

[IV] James A. Garfield, (20th president), Ibid

[1] Milton Friedman, *Capitalism and Freedom,* (Chicago: University of Chicago Press, 1962), 51, cited in John Taylors, *First Principles,* (New York: W.W. Norton & Company, 2012), 22.

[2] Friedrich Hayak, The Road to Serfdom, 1944, in Bruce Caldwell, *Collected Works of F.A. Hayek,* vol. 2, (Chicago: University of Chicago Press, 1962), 112, cited in Taylors, *First Principles,* 22.

[3] Taylor, *First Principles,* 23-24.

4 Ibid., 106.

5 Ibid., 121-122.

6 Ibid., 123-125.

7 Ibid., 78-80

8 Quote from Thomas Edison taken from the "Quotes" section of http:designjerk.com.

9 Taylor, *First Principles*, 88.

10 Quote by Ronald Reagan on http://www.goodreads.com/author/quotes/3543.Ronald_Reagan.

11 Mark R. Levin, *Ameritopia: The Unmaking of America*, (New York: Thresholds Editions, 2012), 5.

12 Notre Dame Victory March, (parenthesis additions are mine), *Notre Dame Fighting Irish Athletics*, http://www.und.com/nd-fightsong.html.

13 *New Oxford American Dictionary*, 2nd ed. Ed. Erin McKean, (New York: Oxford Press, 2005), Also available at oxfordamericandictionary.com.

14 Thomas Jefferson to Edward Carrington, Paris, (27 May 1788), in *The Papers of Thomas Jefferson*, eds. Julian P. Boyd and Charles T. Cullen, cited by Coburn, *The Debt Bomb*, xii.

15 Thomas Jefferson to Alberto Gallatin, October 1809, "To Albert Gallatin," cited by Coburn, *The Debt Bomb*, xii.

7   Coming out of the Asylum - Simpson & Bowles

I Quote from John Danforth on http://barefootsworld.net/banking-fed-quotes.

II Quote from Henry Hazlitt on http://www.quotationcollection.com/author/Henry_Hazlitt/quotes.

1 Dr. Tom Coburn, *The Debt Bomb*, 155.

2 Ibid., 156.

3 Ibid., 159.

[4] Ibid., 161.

[5] Ibid., 174.

[6] Ibid.

[7] Simpson-Bowles Report, "Moment of Truth," cited by Coburn, *The Debt Bomb*, 193.

[8] C. Eugene Steurle and Stephanie Rennane, "Social Security and Medicare Taxes and Benefits Over a Lifetime," Urban Institute, cited by Coburn, *The Debt Bomb*, 193.

[9] Joe Lieberman at "Coburn-Lieberman press conference on Medicare debt reduction plan," (28 June 2011), cited by Coburn, *The Debt Bomb*, 203.

[10] "Warren Buffett, Alan Simpson, & Erskine Bowles On Fixing the Debt Problem," Transcript, Published, (12 July 2012), cnbc.com/id/48166800.

8 Protecting Government Workers from Bread Lines

[1] George Meany, former president of the AFL-CIO, "Room for Debate," *New York Times*, (16 September 2011), http://www. nytimes.com/roomfordebate/2011/02/18/the-first-blow-against-public-employees/fdr-warned-us-about-public-sector-unions

[II] John Reiniers, "FDR's warning: Public Employee Unions a No-No," *Hernando Today*, (17 October 2010), http://www2. hernandotoday.com/news/hernando-news/2010/oct/17/ha-fdrs-warning-public-employee-unions-a-no-no-ar-291004/.

[1] DeMint, *Now or Never*, 107-108.

[2] Ibid., 108.

[3] Bob Williams, "Why Private Sector Unions Are Much Different Than Government Unions," (7 March 2011), http://www.state-budgetsolutions.org/blog/detail/updated-why-private-sector-unions-are-much-different-than-government-unions.

[4] Ibid.

[5] Ibid.

[6] Ibid.

9   Greed and Snake Oil vs. Honest Profit

[I] Quote from Socrates on http://www.goodreads.com/quotes/tag/greed?page=1,5.

[II] Quote from Thomas Paine on http://brainyquote.com/quotes/authors/t/thomas_paine.

[III] Quote from Dan B. Allender on http://modernservantleader.com/resources/leadership-quotes.

[IV] Quote from Margaret Thatcher on http://listverse.com/2007/12/21/top-25-quotes-of-margaret-thatcher/.

[1] Proverbs 24:27 TLB

[2] Proverbs 24:3 TLB

[3] Proverbs 15:27 NCV

[4] Steve Jobs cited by Maria Linn, "What Steve Jobs Taught Us About Life and Money," *Learnvest*, (6 October 2011), http://www.learnvest.com/2011/10/what-steve-jobs-taught-us-about-life-and-money-182/.

[5] Corey Kilgannon, "Serpico on Serpico," *New York Times*, (22 January 2010), http://nytimes.com/2010/01/24/nyregion/24serpico.

[6] "Who Pays Income Taxes and How Much?" *National Taxpayers Union*, (2009), http://ntu.org/tax-basics/who-pays-income-taxes.html.

[7] Tino Sanandaji and Arvid Malm, "Obama's Folly: Why Taxing the Rich Is No Solution," *The American*, (16 August 2011), http://american.com/archive/2011/august/obamasfollytaxingtherich/.

[8] Abraham Lincoln's first inaugural address, (4 March 1861).

10 Those Stubborn Facts and Stats—American Education

[I] Quote from John Chubb and Terry Moe, Brookings Institution Scholars, (1990), http://angelfire.com/mn/rongstadliberty/EducationQuotes.html.

[II] Carolyn Lochhead, Ibid.

[III] Albert Shanker during his time as head of the American Federation of Teachers, Ibid.

[1] Ziglar, *See You at the Top*, 206.

[2] Bill and Melinda Gates, cited by Friedman and Mandelbaum, *That Used To Be Us: How America Fell Behind in the World It Invented and How We Can Come Back*, (New York: Farrar, Straus and Giroux, 2011), 109.

[3] Eric A. Hanushek, a senior fellow at Stanford University's Hoover Institution, cited by Friedman and Mandelbaum, *That Used To Be Us*, 109-110.

[4] Ibid., 110.

[5] Ibid.

[6] OECD PISA 2009 database, cited by Friedman and Mandelbaum, That Used To Be Us, 104.

[7] Ibid., 106.

[8] Chester E. Finn Jr., *New York Times*, (7 December 2010), cited by Friedman and Mandelbaum, *That Used To Be Us*, 104-105.

[9] Susan Engel, director of the teaching program at Williams College, author of *Red Flags or Red Herrings? Predicting Who Your Child Will Become*, cited by Friedman and Mandelbaum, *That Used To Be Us*, 105-106.

[10] Heidrick & Struggles, in partnership with *The Economist*'s intelligence unit, cited by Friedman and Mandelbaum, *That Used To Be Us*, 100.

[11] Senator Jim DeMint, *Now or Never*, (New York: Hatchette Book Group, 2012), 161.

[12] Veronique de Rugy, "Losing the Brains Race," *Reason.com,* (March 2011), http://reason.com/archives/2011/02/22/losing-the-brains-race.

[13] John Stossel, "The Education Blob," *Creators.com,* (4 July 2012), http://www.creators.com/opinion/john-stossel/the-education-blob.html.

[14] DeMint, *Now or Never,* 163-164.

[15] Andrew J. Coulson, "Comparing Public, Private, and Market Schools: The International Evidence," *Cato Institute,* (2009), http://cato.org/pubs/articles/coulson comparing public private market schools jsc.pdf.

[16] "Survey Finds Public Likes School Choice, Private Schools," *CAPE.* (December 1999), http://www.capenet.org/pdf/Outlook250.pdf.

[17] Ibid.

[18] Ibid.

[19] Robert Kennedy, "5 More Reasons Why You Should Consider Private School," *About.com,* http://privateschool.about.com/cs/choosingaschool/a/choice1

11 The Rich, Poor, and Unfortunate Folks in the Middle

[i] Quote from Lew Rockwell on http://www.quotationcollection.com/tag/free%20enterprise/quotes.

[ii] Quote from Sallust (86 BC) Roman Politician, Rose Williams, *Latin Quips at Your Fingertips,* (New York: Fall River Press, 2000), LX.

[iii] Quote from Ronald Reagan on http://www.quotationcollection.com/tag/free%20enterprise/quotes.

[i] "Who Doesn't Pay Federal Taxes?" *Urban Institute and Brookings Institution,* cited by Coburn, *The Debt Bomb,* 240 (see chap. 5, n. 6).

² Jacob Goldstein, "The 47 Percent, In One Graphic," *NPR*, (26 September 2012), http://www.npr.org/blogs/money/2012/09/18/161337343/the-47-percent-in-one-graphic.

³ Coburn, *The Debt Bomb*, 240.

⁴ DeMint, *Now or Never*, 107.

⁵ Rick Joyner, *I See A New America*, (Fort Mill: Quest Ventures, 2011), Kindle Edition.

⁶ DeMint, *Now or Never*, 107.

⁷ Coburn, *The Debt Bomb*, 246.

⁸ Quote from James Madison on http://www.goodreads.com/author/quotes/63859.James_Madiso.n

⁹ Jim DeMint, *Saving Freedom: We Can Stop America's Slide into Socialism*, (Nashville: Fidelis Books, 2009), 43.

¹⁰ Quote from James Madison on http://foundersquotes.com/quotes/i-own-myself-the-friend-to-a-very-free-system-of-commerce-and-hold-it-as-a-truth/#more-918.

12 The Super-Sizing of Government Programs

ᴵ Quote from Martin Luther King Jr. on http://wwwangelfire.com/mn/rongstadliberty/EducationQuotes.

ᴵᴵ John Stuart Mill, Ibid.

ᴵᴵᴵ William Bennett, *Living Out of Sync*, http://fragmentsweb.org/TXT1/synctx.

ᴵ "Milestone Documents in the National Archives," (Washington, DC: National Archivers and Records Administrations, 1995), 69-73, cited by DeMint, *Now or Never*, 72 (see chapt. 5, n. 15).

² DeMint, *Now or Never*, 72.

³ "Milestone Documents in the National Archives," 69-73, cited by DeMint, *Now or Never*, 73.

⁴ Ibid., 74.

[5] Andrew Napolitano, Fox News™ legal analyst, cited by DeMint, *Now or Never*, 75.

[6] Ibid.

[7] DeMint, *Now or Never*, 79.

[8] Ibid., 80-81.

[9] "FDR Takes United States Off Gold Standard." *History.com*, (5 June 1933), http://history.com/this-day-in-history/fdr-takes-united-states-off-gold-standard.

[10] DeMint, *Now or Never*, 81-82.

[11] Ibid., 82.

[12] Joe Kernen and Blake Kernen, *Your Teacher Said What?!: Defending Our Kids from the Liberal Assault on Capitalism*, (New York: Sentinel Penguin Group, 2011), inside cover.

[13] Ibid., x-xi.

[14] Ibid., inside cover.

[15] Quote from Ronald Reagan on http://www.goodreads.com/author/quotes/3543.Ronald_Reagan.

[16] Bill O'Reilly, *Culture Warrior*, (New York: Broadway Books, 2006), 123.

[17] Ibid., 124.

[18] Ibid.

[19] Ibid., 124-125.

[20] Sean Hannity, *Let Freedom Ring—Winning the War of Liberty Over Liberalism*, (New York: HarperCollins Publishers, 2002), 142.

[21] Ziglar, *See You at the Top*, 66.

13 Restoring Dignity and Self-Respect to the Low Income— Real Fairness

[1] Quote from Plato, found on http://www.goodreads.com/ quotes/tag/fairness.

[II] Aristotle, Ibid.

[III] Victor Hugo, Ibid.

[IV] Proverbs 26:25 KJV.

[V] Quote from Benjamin Disraeli on http://www.angelfire.com/ mn/rongstadliberty/EducationQuotes.

[1] "2012 World Hunger and Poverty Facts and Statistics," *WorldHunger.org*, http://www.worldhunger.org/articles/ Learn/world%20hunger%20facts%202002.htm.

[2] Michael David Smith, "Roger Goodell 'Certain' That Regular Refs Are 'Ready to Go,'" *NBC Sports*, (27 September 2012), http://profootballtalk.nbcsports.com/2012/09/27/roger-goodell-certain-that-regular-refs-are-ready-to-go/.

[3] Luke 12:48 KJV

[4] Acemoglu and Robinson, *Why Nations Fail*, 45-46.

[5] Ibid., 68.

[6] Muhammad Yunus, *Banker to the Poor*, (New York: PublicAffairs, 1999), vii-viii.

[7] Ibid., ix.

[8] Ibid., 182.

[9] Ibid., 57-58.

[10] Don Rowland, "Jimmy and Raymond at School," *The Christian Informer*, (July 1998), cited by David Limbaugh, *Persecution— How Liberals are Waging War Against Christianity*, (Washington DC: Regnery Publishing, Inc., 2003), 6.

[11] Ibid.

[12] Josh McDowell and Bob Hostetler, *The New Tolerance, How a Cultural Movement Threatens to Destroy You, Your Faith, and*

Your Children, (Wheaton: Tyndale House Publishers, Inc., 1998), 7, cited by Limbaugh, *Persecution,* 6.

[13] Quote by Ronald Reagan on http://www.goodreads.com/author/quotes/3545.Ronald_Reagan.

[14] Roberts v. Madigan, 921 F.2d 1047 (10th Cir. 1990), cited by Limbaugh, *Persecution,* 6.

[15] Limbaugh, *Persecution,* 7.

[16] Romans 16:17 PHILLIPS

[17] Quote from Ronald Reagan on http://www.humanevents.com/2006/09/06/.

[18] Tom Coburn, *The Debt Bomb,* 280.

[19] Quote from Frederic Bastiat on http://www.safetyhammock.com/2012/05/demerits-of-welfare-state.html

[20] Thomas Jefferson, Ibid.

[21] Thomas Paine, Ibid.

14 Can America Make a Fourth-Quarter Comeback?

[I] Quote from Winston Churchill on http://paragonality.com/2012/07/31/some-assorted-winston-churchill-quotes-on-free-enterprise/.

[II] Quote from Thomas Paine on http://www.brainyquote.com/quotes/authors/t/thomas_paine.

[III] Quote from Aleksandr Solzhenitsyn on http://www.goodreads.com/author/quotes/10420.Aleksandr_I_Solzhenitsyn.

[IV] Quote from Alexis de Tocqueville on http://www.goodreads.com/author/quotes/465.Alexis_de_Tocqueville.

[1] Walter Isaacson, *Steve Jobs,* (New York: Simon & Schuster, 2011), audio edition read by Dylan Baker.

[2] "Franklin's Appeal for Prayer at the Constitutional Convention," http://wallbuilders.com/libissuearticles.asp?id=98.

3 "The Bible—Quotes from Famous Men," *why-the-bible.com,* http://why-the-bible.com/bible.htm.

4 Ibid.

5 Ibid.

6 "Presidents and the Bible," *biblein90days.org,* http://www. biblein90days.org/en/quotes/search.asp?category=Presidents +and+the+Bible.

7 "The Bible—Quotes from Famous Men," *why-the-bible.com,* http://why-the-bible.com/bible.htm.

8 "Presidents and the Bible," *biblein90days.org,* http://www. biblein90days.org/en/quotes/search.asp?category=Presidents +and+the+Bible.

9 Ibid.

10 Ibid.

11 Ibid.

12 Ibid.

13 Ibid.

14 Ibid.

15 Carol Kelly-Gangi, ed., *The Essential Wisdom of the Presidents,* (New York: Fall Press, 2010), 7.

16 Ibid.

17 Ibid., 8.

18 Ibid., 9.

19 Ronald Reagan, "America Is a Shining City Upon a Hill," *SourceWatch,* http://www.sourcewatch.org/index.php?title= America_is_a_shining_city_upon_a_hill.

20 Winston Churchill cited by Robert G. Wright, Director American Anti-Cancer Institute, *Killing Cancer—Not People,* (2011), 35.

21 Elvis Presley, Ibid.

[22] Thomas Jefferson, Ibid., 36.

[23] Albert Einstein, Ibid., 35.

[24] Ronald Reagan, "Shining City," http://www.sourcewatch.org/index.php?title=America_is_a_shining_city_upon_a_hill.

About the Author

Michael J. Muccio first began to develop his keen business sense delivering newspapers at the tender age of eight. As a teenager, he took a job working in the hotel industry and a string of professional successes soon followed, culminating with him managing a top Vegas-style nightclub when he was just nineteen years old. Michael would later go on to establish himself as a leading sales and marketing expert in the corporate world, before finally launching his own consulting company which specialized in training leaders and salespeople in various small businesses and hotels.

After serving as a volunteer for a campaign for Frank Keating, who eventually became a two term governor, Michael met with Jack Kemp. This meeting inspired him to become even more involved in his local community, and he was soon sponsoring debates for local candidates, interfacing with elected leaders, and serving on a special civic committee.

Over the years, Michael has had a tremendous impact on hundreds of small businesses across America, improving their productivity and inspiring countless American workers to achieve their personal and professional goals. Fueled by Michael's passion for excellence in business and his interest in the political arena, *America's Battle for Free Enterprise* was birthed out of a larger research project that spanned nearly a decade. Today Michael travels and speaks to businesses, schools, non-profit organizations, and churches.

You may contact the author at:

mjmuccio@gmail.com

americas-battle.com